FROM MANHATTAN
TO THE HOLY MOUNTAIN
OF ATHOS

ORTHODOX LOGOS PUBLISHING

FROM MANHATTAN TO THE HOLY MOUNTAIN OF ATHOS
A TRUE STORY
THE HERO RECOUNTS

by Thodoris Spiliotis

Editing by Giorgos Proestos, Christina Kyriakidou and Kevin Custers

Publishers Maxim Hodak & Max Mendor

© 2024, Thodoris Spiliotis

© 2024, Orthodox Logos Publishing,

The Netherlands

www.orthodoxlogos.com

ISBN: 978-1-80484-142-6
ISBN: 978-1-80484-143-3

This book is in copyright. No part of this publication may be reproduced, stored in a retrieval system or transmitted in any form or by any means without the prior permission in writing of the publisher, nor be otherwise circulated in any form of binding or cover other than that in which it is published without a similar condition, including this condition, being imposed on the subsequent purchaser.

FROM MANHATTAN TO THE HOLY MOUNTAIN OF ATHOS

ORTHODOX LOGOS PUBLISHING

The book is dedicated to the hero of the true story and all those who disregarded everything in order to dedicate themselves, body and soul, to what they love and their hearts dictate, ignoring the Laistrygonians and Cyclops.

AUTHOR'S NOTE

When a person decides to get to know – and not simply to visit out of tourist or pilgrimage interest – the Athonian Community, he will realize that the experience of this meeting will never end. There is always something left. Something starts. Something continues. It is an open invitation to new knowledge, a new experience, a new story.

That is how the story of the *Monk who became a CEO* started a few years ago – it was born from a quest for knowledge, through the puzzlement about the excellent and effective organization of the Athonian Community. However, when knowledge is acquired, it must then be shared, be socially useful, have social impact, and leave its marks on society.

Every story always teaches, puzzles, and sheds light. It lights new thought paths, usually unseen until we listen to it or read about it. It awakens. It transforms.

The monk who became CEO highlighted the principles of Athonian management as time-tested principles of successful management born from a thousand years of practical application.

Four years after the publication and distribution of Athonian knowledge throughout the many branches of business, I would be deeply grateful if my first book managed to re-direct the organization and focus of a modern business towards substantially human-oriented and utilitarian axes.

Knowledge, however, is a chain. There is always consecutive knowledge, which, like a safety link, complements and strengthens the already existing cognitive chain. Like such a knowledge link, a new story now takes its place in the chain.

The core subject and basic material of the new book you are holding in your hands is the true life of a man who, for years, had been facing his ambitions, anxieties, scruples and uncertainties, until he heard his inner voice clearly and followed it, until he found his destination and met essential happiness.

A true story, however, is by itself not enough to arouse the readers' interest, if it lacks honest humanitarian destination, if it cannot help people enhance their inner strength, take a step forward, re-determine their comfort zone and proceed in their lives with more secure steps.

Life is, after all, like a pair of shoes. The more comfortable we feel inside them, the more enjoyable the walk will be.

Enjoy reading!
Thodoris Spiliotis

The main character today lives on Mount Athos

For reasons of privacy, his real name is not mentioned in the text. The same is true for the names of the co-protagonists of the story (or some of them).

After all, what is interesting about the narrative of true events is the human actions and behaviors, life choices and teachings, and not the persons themselves.

New York, January, 2020
New York University,
Auditorium, Honors Hall

"The President of the University is requested to take the floor, give the welcoming address and announce the guest of honor."

"Dear students, I am impressed by your presence in today's special event. More than a thousand students are in the hall at this moment. We tried to cover the request for seats for everybody. Some are unfortunately standing. We ask for your understanding and patience.

To be honest with you, I was not expecting such participation. Your interest was probably aroused by the guest's personality, his status, or both. It is not the first time we have invited a graduate of our university in order to honor him for his life and outstanding activity since graduation. It is not the first time an important person's achievements have their origin here, in these rooms, in this very auditorium. In a few minutes from now the trajectory of an exceptionally interesting life will unfold before our eyes, and I really wish that it may, through its teachings and references, serve as a beacon for all of us.

This is a special year, a milestone for our university. By invitation of the Senate, there is among us a graduate who no longer lives in the USA. He is an American and Greek citizen who, today, lives in the only self-governed part of Greece, on Mount Athos. The invitation, which was easy and unanimous to decide, was difficult and time-consuming to accept for purely procedural reasons. But still, the formal difficulties were overcome in a few months, thanks to the common willingness for this meeting and honest and mutual good will. I am hoping that the narration of our guest's life will makes us all understand that a person who has chosen to dedicate himself to the spiritual life, justifiably and consciously distances himself from anything to do with the world. This is exactly what amplifies our joy and honor for having him here among us today.

I could talk for hours about this man who decided to leave America more than 37 years ago, leaving everything behind in terms of routine and his general way of life, and has since lived in a quiet place of unique natural beauty in northern Greece, untouched by human hands, on a peninsula with an imposing mountain, Athos, known as the Holy Mount. We are, therefore, looking forward to listening to this man's life story. The story of "the happiest person in the world," as the biggest American newspaper called him recently, here to share his wisdom with us. I believe that his figure already stands out in our packed auditorium. A figure that has already lit the faces of all of us with optimism and serenity.

We welcome you, father, in the corridors and halls of our university, where you have walked for years in your student years. Today in particular, we welcome you in this Auditorium in the "Honors Hall." The entire Senate, but above all our students, are waiting impatiently to hear you.

Dear students, I am almost certain you will want to ask questions during the speech. Our distinguished guest is willing to accept and answer all of them. After all, dialogue has, over time, been better than monologue. The floor is yours."

"I honestly do not know how to start. I confess that this is the first time in my life that I am speaking from the pulpit and I will not hide that I am already nervous. I wish to publicly express my surprise and gratitude for the honor of being invited here today. I feel, however, that I do not deserve something so special; nor does my way of life justify the expectation of such recognition. What finally imposed my presence here was not my value, but your kindness and love, be assured of that. I will start, therefore, with this public confession and proceed by expressing my sincere gratitude. I would have preferred my speech to have been in Greek, as spiritual concepts are more accurately expressed in the Greek language and would have had a greater effect and be better understood, but alas.

I am deeply moved as, after almost four decades, I am visiting the academic environment which nurtured me, educated me, provided me with knowledge, turned me into a man and gave me the possibility and the wings to navigate through life, having first come into contact with the meritocratic system of America. I feel certain that, if my life had not passed through the streets and avenues of Manhattan, its course would have been entirely different. The city where I spent sixteen wonderful years has changed my life's orientation. I walked today in the streets of New York and memories of an intense student life with carelessness, hard work, smiles, anxieties, rewards, interviews, and disappointments came back to me. It is a foretaste of the life that follows. I visited my old neighborhood, and automatically my body and mind were filled with memories and feelings, as though I had not been away for even a day.

I want to thank all of you for being here today, and especially the rector for the honorable invitation. I have been preparing my speech for some time and I will not conceal my anxiety. Forgive my accent. My absence during all these years is certainly no help. I am living in a place where only Greek can be heard, from all stages of development of the Greek language: modern spoken Greek, purist Greek, official liturgical Greek, common Greek, the Hellenistic language of the Apostle Paul, even the ancient Greek of Aristotle.

Forgive me, Mr. rector, members of the Senate, dear students, for my doubts regarding my presence here today. The reason for my doubts can be summarized in just one sentence:

> *I wish that my presence here is not*
> *Transformed in presence of the Ego*

Never in my life had I thought that I would become a monk, because I did not actually know what monasticism was. I will transport you several decades back in Athens, Greece. In the mid-1050s my large family is ready to welcome its new member. The arrival of the last-born is a great blessing, as the ninth child of the family will see the light of day. That is how my life starts in the center of Athens, the capital of Greece. The preoccupation of our parents to provide their children with social and academic education, morals and values, in order to respond to the social needs of the time, was mandatory, as it always is. The struggle of the head of the family was even harder in order to raise us in dignity. My parents were very pious and raised us during that time with spiritual values, endowing us with unforgettable moments and experiences, despite the minor revolts of our childhood and adolescence. At school I was a good student, but an unruly one at the same time. I was drawn by trouble, a restless spirit. I remember that even then theoretical sciences were not my thing…

A dilemma before the decision
Thursday, 23 August 1973, Athens

Time flew and the school years passed. As soon as I finished the Lyceum, I took part in the admission exams and I was ready to study in the National Technical University of Athens.

I had to make a decision regarding my future. There was no time to lose. During that period, my older brother Spyros was studying for his post-graduate degree in Business Administration (MBA) at the New York University (NYU). Lefteris, who is very much familiar with Universities, as well as life in America, encouraged me to also go to New York.

"Congratulations, Peter, for your exceptional performance. You managed to get admitted to one of the most historical and best academic institutions. However, I have my doubts. There is great instability in the country."

"What do you mean, Lefteris? As the older one, you must know something."

"I don't know if it is good for you to stay in an uncertain future."

"And what are you proposing? Do you have an alternative?" I asked.

"The one and only solution is for you to go and find our brother and study in the land of opportunity."

"I was admitted to one of the best schools. Isn't it a pity if I abandon the vindication of so much effort and sacrifice?"

"The situation is out of control. There are rumors that the Universities will not open in the new year. The students will occupy them" he said.

"It is hard for me to leave, Lefteris, leave our family, our brothers and sisters, our friends, and go to an unknown country. Moreover, I do not speak English well."

"Perhaps we should call Spyros in the afternoon, discuss the matter and ask for his opinion?"

"Agreed, but I can tell you right now that I am against it."

"It is best to call late in the evening. He will be back from work then," decided Lefteris, and that is what we did.

"Good evening, Spyros dear!"

"Pete, my beloved! How nice to hear from you! How is everyone in Greece?"

"We are all well."

"How did you do in the exams?"

"I was admitted to the Mechanical Engineers' School in the National Technical University."

"Bravo! Congratulations!" he cried excitedly. "What made you call me so soon? We spoke nearly a week ago. Has something happened since?"

"No, but the way things are, something will happen. Wait a minute, I will pass you to Lefteris who wants to speak to you."

"Hallo, Lefteris, how are you?"

"We are all well, thank God. Everybody says hello, especially mother. Things in Greece are unstable and I called you to discuss whether it is good for Pete to go to the Technical University or to come to you over there."

"Listen, Lefteris, life here is difficult and molded, but – as you yourself know thanks to your studies in England and

America – the system is fair and meritocratic. Those who try are rewarded. You also know very well that life here is expensive in comparison to Greece. If Pete comes to New York he will have to work. All students do, to tell the truth. What do our parents say about your thoughts?"

"Spyros, we have the experience of studies and life in America. That is why I called you and not our father. It will certainly be a difficult decision for our family, but if there is no other choice!... Can we find out if registrations for the first year are finished at your university? If they are, then Pete will obviously stay here and we will act according to the current situation."

"Ok, Lefteris. I will ask tomorrow at the university secretariat and let you know."

Following day, New York, 09.00 am
New York University, Students' Desk

"Good morning. I would like some information about admissions, please. My name is Spyros Ioannidis and I'm a post-graduate student at the university. I'm interested in registrations for first-year students, specifically my brother, at the Faculty of Mechanical Engineering."

"Good morning, Mr. Ioannidis! Registrations at the university close in fourteen days for first-year students for all University Faculties. The registration deadline is the 7th of September. Your brother, therefore, has 14 days to submit the required documents. Then he will be called to pass some exams."

"Thank you for the information. My brother lives in Greece and I'm afraid it is rather difficult for us to make the submission deadlines."

"I cannot interfere with deadlines. Sorry."

Athens, 05.30 pm

"Answer the phone! It is probably Spyros," my brother said to me.

"You answer it, Lefteris! I do not want to go to the USA, anyway."

"Good afternoon, Lefteris! Today I visited the Students' Desk and they told me that we have 14 days to submit the documents, which must of course be translated. If your decision is final, we must hurry."

"We will prepare the documents immediately. I will talk to our parents and we will inform you. I believe our brother's future is there, with you. Good evening." Lefteris hung up and turned to me. "We must collect the papers. Pete, tomorrow you will go to the Ministry of Foreign Affairs for the translations."

"What do you think, father?" I asked our father.

"Your brothers are experienced and they know what is best for your future," he said. "My son, as your parents, we will support you as best we can."

"Ok, father, ok, Lefteris. Since you believe it is the best choice, I will go. You have the experience and father has the wisdom, and you certainly want what is best for me. So, I will obey and prepare for the trip."

At the last minute they accepted the documents and they asked me to travel to America to take the entrance exams. It was the main condition for admittance.

I prepared my suitcases in a few days, as I had been given a specific exam date and there was no way to postpone the journey.

At some point, my mother called me into the bedroom.

"My son, from now on, the Virgin will be your mother in the place you are going to, and whatever you ask for with faith and passion with all your heart, she will give to you generously. Take this small icon of the Virgin with you."

"Thank you very much, mother. I will put it up in my room and plead to it. I will put it in my suitcase on top of everything; this way, it will be the first thing I take out when I arrive."

I had just reached 18 years of age and was travelling for the first time outside of Greece by plane, on my own, on such a long journey, not knowing what my future had in store for me.

Departure to the future
Sunday 9 September, 1973
New York, JFK Airport

"My brother, what a pleasure to see you! It has been over three years."

"Pete, welcome to the world's metropolis!"

"This airport is huge! I have never seen so many terminals and so many people walking around an airport."

"How was your trip?"

"As a first-time trip by air, it was tiresome. It was a long trip."

"You seem to be enchanted. Let's go get the car in the parking lot and drive to my place and you can tell me your impressions later."

Lost in the world's metropolis, among unknown people, I cannot get enough of seeing the streets of Manhattan with the tall buildings and huge avenues. I inhale energy instead of air.

New York, 31st Street
5th Avenue and Broadway

We arrive home. To my surprise, we go to the top floor of a very tall building. My brother knew the janitor who was Greek and had given it to him at a very low rent for the period.

"This is the apartment, little brother, which from today on will serve as shelter for the both of us. Tomorrow, you take the admissions exams at the university. We must rest, so that you'll perform as best you can. Concentrate and write well, otherwise your trip will end prematurely. If all goes well – which I hope it will – we will have plenty of time to walk around New York."

"The apartment is nothing like our home in Greece. I still have to come to grips with where I am. I will go to bed and relax, so I can take the exams in the morning as rested as possible."

Automatically, all the images I collected throughout the day come to mind. Unknown experiences for me. Another world, different customs and behaviors, different people. I have no time to process it all. They are the first images of the start of a new life.

The jet-lag keeps me from sleeping at all. In the morning, I get up truly lost and exhausted.

Monday 10th September, 1973
New York University

I arrive at the university stressed and clearly unprepared. My only real support in New York is my brother. I start with the written exam and then the oral one. Whatever I know of the language is what I learned at school and from some English books I'd read in the previous years.

"Do you think I can make it, Spyros?" I ask insecurely.

"I know the examiners are demanding, but fair. I understand your stress, but everything will go well. Try to do your best."

In the written exam, the questions seemed relatively easy to me. But, to be honest, I found the orals difficult. In Greece the level of knowledge regarding the scientific direction is on average quite high. Perhaps that is the reason why I managed to meet the demands.

Monday 17th September, 1973
New York, Manhattan, 31st Street, Apartment 6b

I am anxiously awaiting the results. I feel excited at the prospect of studying here and entering a new phase of my life. The negative disposition I had before leaving Greece has disappeared.

"Good morning, sir. Can I please talk to Mr. Peter Ioannidis?" I hear an unknown voice at the other end of the line.

"It is me. Who is it, please?"

"I am calling from the university secretariat. You can come by to get the exam results from the Students' Desk."

"Do you know them?" I ask anxiously.

"They are confidential, Mr. Ioannidis. I cannot give them to you over the phone."

I get dressed quickly and run out. I am really anxious to get the results. Knowledge has always fascinated me and I wanted to use it. I arrive almost out of breath and I take the envelope they give me. I open it impatiently and read the document that contains my successful admittance to the first year of the Faculty of Mechanical Engineering.

I am overcome with excitement, but at the same time I think it is impossible for me to expect money from my father for my studies. My family's needs are great. Our family members are numerous and I do not want to live at the expense of others. I came here to further myself, to create, to strive, because only by overcoming difficulties will one understand what ordinary life means.

Life gets meaning in difficult conditions

I must find work immediately.

As soon as I return home, I realize that I am starting a new life, which I had never planned or imagined. *Has fortune brought me here?* I ask myself.

Whatever it was that brought me here, I must bow my head and persevere. in my mind I can hear the words of the great Greek author Nikos Kazantzakis:

"Do not deign to ask: "Shall we win? Shall we be defeated?" Fight!"

Alone at home. My brother is finishing up on his post-graduate degree. He has his final exams and then has to finish the thesis. He has a lot of studying to do and, although he has a scholarship from the university, he needs to work somewhere, particularly during the weekends, in order to cover his expenses. He is working as maître d' at the Sirocco Supper Club at 29th Street in Manhattan.

I am thinking that, in a few days time, I will start my school as a "freshman." An unprecedented experience. Everything is new – new people, new friends. I definitely need to adapt and socialize in order to make it.

The adaptation is proceeding smoothly through the process of finding work and my daily contact with the New York society. I do not deny that I am missing my family and friends and so I let the first tears flow: homesickness and solitude.

Since Spyros is away and it is quiet, I am thinking that it is an opportunity for me to improve my English. Before beginning, I start taking my clothes out of the suitcases. It is a message to myself that there is no turning back. I cannot look back. My present and future are here. I made a decision and I will stand by it.

We have a bedroom that we share and a common desk for studying. In addition, Spyros has left me a small corner in the room to store my belongings. In the suitcase, on top of everything, is the icon of the Mother Virgin. I hold it in my hands and hang it at a prominent place in the room.

I start reading incessantly, motivated by my new life which calls me to live and get used to it.

> *In life, motivation is necessary, otherwise there can be no advancement or creation.*

I am tired. I take a deep breath and I glance at the icon. I get up, kiss it and tears fill my eyes. I plead to it. *Holy Mother, I have no time to lose. Time is pressing. I have to pay the tuition fees for my school. Please, help me.*

I start crying. I cannot stop weeping. I need to work. There is no possibility for my brother to support me.

I hear keys at the door.

"Hello, Pete, dear. What are you doing? How are you? I have very good news for you. Our mother's blessing worked. I spoke to the man in charge of the night club where I work and tomorrow you can start as an assistant waiter."

"Brother, I want to kiss you! When did you say I could start?"

"Tomorrow at seven."

I'm feeling such a will to work inside me... I have never worked in my life. But I feel a special energy and eagerness.

Sirocco Supper Club, 29th Street, Manhattan, New York, 07.00 pm

I arrive at the club and the moment I enter I hear a melody that is definitely Greek, but with Jewish lyrics. It does not take long for me to realize that the orchestra is playing Manos Hatzidakis and the singer is interpreting the song *Every garden – Shoun elai* in Jewish. I feel proud to be Greek and listen to the great Manos Hatzidakis in the streets of Manhattan.

"Welcome. You are Peter, Spyros's brother, right? You look alike. I am Aris San – Aristidis Seisanas – born in Kalamata and raised in Israel. You must excuse me, but I must accompany my group. The manager will inform and train you. We will talk later."

"Welcome. I am Mike, the restaurant manager. You will do exactly as I say and we will be all right. This work needs alertness, speed and excellent cooperation with the kitchen staff. All tables are by reservation, except the one in the corner which is for our Mafia friends."

We start, but there is no time for training! I have to take the plunge and perform. I cannot hide that it is quite difficult for me. At the beginning I felt I had suddenly entered a different society, totally alien to me. Different people, different characters, different cultures and behaviors; an area which by itself is a life experience.

I am working with great eagerness and enthusiasm. I refuse to even consider failure and this helps me to keep my eyes on the future. I feel that I am taking exams in hard work and good behavior. I can feel it, but I can also see it in my managers as our collaboration progresses.

The Sirocco Supper Club is very popular and people queue up to get a table. It is full every day! Many Hollywood stars are guests: Anthony Quinn, Telly Savalas and Harry Belafonte, while even Stelios Kazantzidis used to sing here at one time. In fact, Manos Hatzidakis made a record in 1975 with the title "A night at Sirocco."

People adore Aris San for his talent and way of playing – "bouzouki style with electric guitar" -, his voice, but mainly for his presence on the scene, his elegant clothes and impressive demeanor. The team consists of musicians of mixed nationalities. Greeks, Israelis and Arabs have created a musical mosaic that enchants with its melodies and creates a unique atmosphere. The environment is friendly, full of Greek and Israeli melodies.

I observe and meet new people, new behaviors. And – most importantly – I'm among people and not isolated in my room. Life always brings us to a point where we have to act, so as not to get trapped in inactivity.

I had not completed a month as assistant waiter and the post of the daily cleaning worker became vacant. They suggested that, if I wanted it, I could cover that post temporarily, as well. They informed me that there would be additional wages for that work. I did not think for long and eagerly accepted the offer, as it would help me get the money for the university tuition fee.

Thursday 25th October, 1973, 04.00 am
Sirocco Supper Club, 29th Street, Manhattan

Today we were so busy that we hardly managed all of the customer's orders. I thought we would never finish. Now, at last, we are picking things up and cleaning up the place, exhausted.

Every time after closing, the bartender Vasilis, who is also Greek, offers to drive me from 29th Street to my apartment on 31st, so that I don't have to walk through the streets of Manhattan alone late at night. He approaches laughing.

"Come on, let's finish up and leave."

4.30 in the morning, I get into his car and we set out to return home. Without saying a word, he takes a different route.

"Where are we going?" I ask.

"You'll see! Don't worry!"

Nearly 15 minutes later, we arrive in front of an iron garage door. At least that is what it looks like to me…

He knocks in a special way and after a moment a small window opens on the top right of the door.

"Vasilis, who's this guy with you?" asks the person who appears in the opening.

"Don't worry, he is my nephew," he answers.

I was scared, as he had not told me where we would go. The door opens and they start frisking us, first Vasilis and then me. This was a first-time experience for me and I am trembling with fear. In the end they let us proceed, after hanging an entrance ticket around our necks.

We first cross an empty, dark room, probably to slowly get us used to the surroundings. We arrive at a huge, double, closed door, where we have to press a button in order to enter. I really have no idea where we are, but I cannot go back.

Suddenly, after the door opens, we find ourselves in a huge hall with velvet carpets, very good lighting in various colors and excellent bass music. I am looking at a small-size casino with many people captivated by their passion of gambling. Without stopping anywhere, we go directly to the dice table.

Vasilis takes a stack of dollars – a lot of money – and places it on the table. When his turn comes, he takes the dice in his hands and throws them.

"Let's go!" he tells me.

"Where are we going?"

"We're leaving."

"And the money you lost, aren't you going to get it back? Won't you break even?"

"Forget it. Sometimes they take your money, sometimes you take theirs. That's life: a lesson for you." And as we speak, we are heading for the exit.

I felt sorry. Within mere seconds, a mere throw of the dice, not only the whole day's wages were lost, but certainly much more. That scene resonated deeply within my heart. I was inexperienced back then. Today I would approach the situation completely differently and I would have answered him, something I did not do then.

Vasilis was only right about one thing: that we need to learn. The wise ancient phrase "Grow older and learn constantly" is always pertinent. We should learn during every second of our lives. Learn from our mistakes and passions which often lead us to situations we cannot easily escape from. Knowledge makes us progress, better understand our environment and the people around us, and it finally helps us to expand our thinking beyond the obvious.

During the next 20 days, the manager promoted me to full-time employee. This development was – I feel – thanks to the zeal and dedication I showed from day one. Perhaps it was something like a reward. Besides, there is no advancement in life without these two basic conditions.

Thanks to this new situation, I now had a better opportunity to save the money required for the first tuition payment.

From the loving arms of my parents and siblings, I was thrown directly into the deep end. But that is life, isn't it? Nothing comes for free. You have to try. Man is made not only to face the easy, but also the difficult. That is why he needs to be prepared for anything.

I am not complaining about what is happening in my life. We must live life as it comes. I was given an opportunity and it was then up to me to make the most of it.

Sunday, 28 April 1974
Party at sundown, Manhattan

After six months and many mental pictures later, time has come to leave my first job. In order to celebrate, we decided with a few other colleagues to go to a party we had been invited to, on a beautiful terrace, just ten minutes outside the city center.

We can see the entire city. Various shades of wonderful colors and lights everywhere on the terrace, but the eye is drawn to the red sunset sky. Hence the name "party at sundown."

I am impressed as I enter. The music is excellent; it sends you to a different place. Unexpected sounds, and the mind is trying to capture everything I see, recording a puzzle of impressions which will turn into experiences and unforgettable memories. Sometimes the mind cannot process everything the eyes see, and so some images settle directly into the soul, unfiltered, and will stay with you forever. The moments are recorded and do not fade. Their color remains permanent.

"Shall we drink some whisky?" I propose. "What do you say? I'm going to the bar to get some. Whisky, anyone?"

"Anything so long as it can be drunk, Peter!"

My eyes are drawn to the entrance, to two breathtakingly beautiful girls joining the party. I have just taken the drinks for me and my friends and approach them without hesitation.

"Would you like a drink?" I ask them. "I am Peter."

"Thank you. Of course, we shall have a drink. We came here to have a good time."

"Join us, let me get the drinks. And allow me to express my admiration."

We are talking and laughing at stories and jokes. I talk about Greece, speaking proudly of my country, its civilization and people, and about my journey to New York. They show great interest – at least I think they do.

"Please excuse us. We'll go inside for a few minutes and then we'll be back. We won't be long."

"Ok, we will talk later." I think they are going to freshen up.

I continue to have a good time with my friends. The girls disappear for quite some time.

After almost 45 minutes, I see them come out smiling and approaching us. I am talking to them, but they cannot utter a word. They try to speak, but let out something of a cry. I cannot understand what is happening, but after a while I realize the effect of drugs on their soul and body. I ask myself for a moment how these substances can destroy two girls, so young and beautiful.

*

Restless, a student raises his hand in the auditorium. He wants to intervene. I am pleased to see interest in the room so soon.

"I would like to hear your question."

"Good afternoon. My name is Paul Maclouis and I am a third-year student in Economics. I would like to ask a question. What do you think led those young girls to drugs? Is age what makes us young people vulnerable to temptation, and how easy is it for us to diverge from our course? Thank you."

"I thank you for the question. You will allow me to make a parenthesis at this point regarding the subject of our life destination and how it is shaped depending on each one's volition and freedom. It is clear that each one of us is free to shape their life as they want and can freely experience it as either heaven or hell on earth. If a person is correctly positioned regarding the destination, meaning for what purpose he is on earth, he can also position himself regarding the individual issues of his life, like his relations to others, his studies, profession, marriage, having children.

In essence, our subconscious life is the one making the critical decisions, as it is guided by the conscious one. The right positioning depends on guidance from selfless people, guided by their love for and from us. At each stage of our life, it is important to have someone who, with undiluted love and interest, shows us the way and the options we have. From then on, it is our own exclusive responsibility to make the right decision and, of course, to assume responsibility for our actions.

There is no decision without responsibility
There is no decision without commitment

However, if we do not assume the right perspective regarding the basic issue of the destination mentioned above, then we will fail with mathematic precision in the individual purposes of our life. Because, what meaning can individual purposes have, when human life as a whole has no destination and meaning? People are ignorant. We believe that our life's purpose is, in the best of cases, the simple moral improvement, to become a better person.

How general!
How hypocritical!

To sum it up, to answer your question, I want to say that those drugs show the lack or loss of orientation those girls had. In our life, in particular in young people's lives, as I said before, guidance serves as a beacon. When it is not there, people function in an uncontrollable manner, choosing the wrong harbors for relief from rough seas. These harbors are these substances, as they purely superficially and misleadingly cover the emotional void young people have, by replacing the lost motivation in their life. In reality, however, they create multiple long-lasting problems for themselves, often without solutions.

As for the second part of your question, it suffices to say that the more unstable our orientation in life is, the more vulnerable we are to aberration and derailing."

You need to get lost in order to find your way

Thursday 2 May, 1974
Sirocco Supper Club

This is officially the last day of my first job. It is time for me to advance, to progress. Every step we make is a sign of development, regardless of success or failure.

I am feeling exhausted, but happy to have had new experiences in such a short time. Towards the end of the evening, as I am picking up empty plates and glasses from the table, suddenly a thin middle-aged man stops me.

"Young man, I would like someone like you to work for my restaurant. Do you know someone?"

I look at him carefully and smiling I say: "I am interested in working myself, but I am studying and I cannot work full-time, only part-time."

"That is exactly what I'm looking for. Come in on Monday and we'll work out the details."

Having passed baptism by fire – I confess, without particular effort – I immediately found work at a steak house, a very expensive one for that time, with high-quality meats and rib eye as a specialty. People from all over New York and elsewhere would come to try out the menu. Sammy's restaurant is in the heart of Manhattan, at the corner of Chrystie and Delancey Str.

My first contact with this region was not the best possible. Sidewalks full of drunk people provide a spectacle that simultaneously invokes sadness and pity. Really hurt people who have nothing to hold onto in life. However, I should not judge, in order to not be judged myself. In life, it serves us well to overlook our neighbors' sins, falls and weaknesses. We do not know what our fellow humans are going through. It is preferable to stand at their side morally and practically as far as possible, instead of judging them. Becoming judges does not make us superior.

I met some of these people and we became friends. I helped them as much as I could. Only when you help and provide, you can understand even a little of the other person's position and pain.

Sammy's Restaurant, 05.00 pm

Monday, the start of a new week and a new start for me. I reach the restaurant by train. At the entrance, my new employer, Sammy, is waiting for me. We sit at a small table in a corner of the restaurant and, while he is informing me about the demands and duties of the work I will undertake, gradually the girls come into the place one by one, greeting him in a familiar way.

"These girls you see are your colleagues. You will share the tips, which as you will see in time, will cover your expectations more than enough."

"Are you sure? Tips divided by five and they will cover our expectations?"

"Do not worry! Believe me!"

Meanwhile, as the hours pass, I remain in the room to get used to things, until the restaurant slowly starts fill up. After introducing my to my new colleagues and as I am just about to leave, Sammy calls me.

"Peter, there is one basic condition in order to employ you as a permanent member of staff."

"Certainly, let's hear it."

"We will start at twice a week and we'll see how it goes from there."

"I can only make it on weekends."

"I have no objection to that."

As I am going to catch my train, I think that although the new job does not present significant progress in my professional development, at least – in comparison to my previous job – I have been promoted. From assistant waiter to waiter.

The important thing is for you to feel useful where you are

I start work in the first weekend and I confirm to myself that I am a communicative person. I like the interaction with the customers and especially the cooperation with my colleagues. There is a spirit of cooperation and comradeship which translates into efficiency, as harmony among colleagues is one of the fundamental conditions of productivity.

Sammy is scanning all of my movements, behavior, and my cooperation with the kitchen staff. He observes my chemistry with the chef, the way I serve food, but also my behavior towards customers. An employee must have more than one skill, in order to fulfill his duties adequately and successfully. If one chooses progress over stagnation and complacency, life never stops being a struggle for the acquisition of new experiences and skills.

I realize that he is monitoring me, which I think makes sense. I am simply being myself. I always have a generous smile on my face, which I feel is an important characteristic to conquer people's hearts, whether they are friends, partners, or customers. That is my character: open, extrovert, perhaps even effusive. I do my job with zeal and I am pleased to feel that I am succeeding, because success is a commitment to ourselves.

On the other hand, there is no plan B, no alternative in case of failure, as the only thing I can do is to succeed – that's how I define success. Success is a one-way street, not necessarily as a result, but as a race and a course. It is a relative term, a text open to many interpretations.

After three weekends of work, Sammy calls me.

"You are good at what you do, but I want to see what other skills you have. When are you free to come by?"

"How about on Wednesday around one?"

And so I did. I go into the restaurant and what do I see? The four waitresses auditioning in front of a microphone.

"Peter, I want you to sing joyful Greek songs that have rhythm. This will be your show during the evening. Things are simple. During your break you will sing. I want you to excite the customers. I want them to break plates!"

"Sammy, I have never sung in my life."

"Come on, it's nothing! Do you know that gentleman?"

"Of course! It's Tuvia Toll."

"You will have a couple of rehearsals with him and you will succeed. Tuvia knows the lyrics to all Greek songs."

I am not prepared, but still I like the idea of having a break from serving and entertaining the customers.

Before making a decision, let us ask ourselves:
Am I ready for the consequences of my decision?

In any case, I can say I have – or at least am trying to have – an artist's style. I have shoulder-length hair. I am full of youth, freshness and energy. I like myself – if I can say so – regarding my appearance, but I control my vanity, or at least I am trying. I take care of my appearance using my new "profession" as an excuse.

The first song that came to mind for the rehearsal was *Dirlada* the most famous Greek song at the time. We all got into the rhythm immediately and connected. We chose more Greek and Spanish songs of the time, and so I would sing for about 20 minutes. And at the end, a surprise.

We've already had some rehearsals with Tuvia and found out that I am not out of tune, at least. That's quite something! Each of the four girls has her own show. Two are singing, one dances and one does imitations.

I am ready to start my new career. You never know where life will lead you...

Saturday night. The restaurant is full. Sammy presents me to the customers for the first time:

"Today, I would like to present to you, for the first time, Mr. Petros Ioannidis, the Greek, who came directly from Athens to sing especially for you."

Strong applause and cheers follow. I step onto a small platform where the piano used to be, and Tuvia and I start our repertoire.

The first song, as in the rehearsals, is *OH, dirlada, dirladada.* Together with the audience, we sing and clap our hands. Then, the waitresses and I dance hasaposerviko in the middle of the hall. We stop serving and start dancing. We present a small show, which causes great enthusiasm.

Among the restaurant's customers are famous actors, singers, businesspeople who all very much enjoy this alternative program. Until then I had no idea that Greek music had such an appeal and excited people so much. The restaurant was a hangout for Paul Newman, Frank Sinatra, Steve McQueen.

The last song I used to sing was Frank Sinatra's legendary *My way.* One night, after finishing my program, I went to serve at the table where Frank Sinatra was sitting, without having seen him. I froze, but I saw him smiling to me and was relieved. I never learned whether he had heard me sing that night or had arrived later. His smile, however, was balm on my soul.

What a guy Sammy was! He had a waiter and singer in one, with no additional fee. Two birds with one stone.

Mother, what a pity you cannot see me! I am a singer now!

I confess that as a group we are very successful and customers enjoy themselves very much, even famous ones. We must not forget that they, too, need to blow off steam, as they have passions and weaknesses too, like all of us. We often tend to turn persons into gods, and consider them superior to the standards and voids of our own lives. However, with the same unconsidered thought and ease, we often demystify and belittle what we had, until yesterday, praised with passion and enthusiasm. Human weaknesses make no exceptions. They are all part of human nature, and that is why they are called human. What differs from person to person is the intensity and their way of management.

So here we are, I have become a singer! By chance, as we say. However, this experience was not wasted. It helped me greatly with was about to come.

In this restaurant I also meet the first love of my life, a waitress and member of the group with which we sing. She is an American and helps me understand and assimilate American culture faster, but also to improve my English. God helps those who help themselves.

Two years later, in the streets of Manhattan

The years go by and I am starting to feel at home in New York. I am doing very well at the university and I'm particularly interested in the engineering sector. I attend the courses with motivation and enthusiasm and pass my exams relatively easily.

We have formed a close-knit student's group. We usually meet at the university and, after our courses, we walk through the streets of Manhattan, as we only have enough money for the bare necessities. Walking is a cost-free solution, after all. I love the area, and for this reason I continue to live in Manhattan, even after my brother's return to Greece, in a small but pleasant apartment on 32nd Street.

With my friends we often visit the Greek neighborhood, Astoria, where many students live, as rents there are much cheaper than in Manhattan. The environment in Astoria is intensely reminiscent of Greece. There are Greek stores everywhere. Astoria is a live flame of the Greek nation, kept burning for decades. The Greek community keep unaltered customs and traditions which we might no longer find in Greece.

One of my close friends is Yiorgos, whom I met at the university. He comes to Manhattan almost every weekend for brunch. He lives in Astoria and for that specific weekend we had agreed that I would pick him up at his place, go for our customary walk and drink our beloved coffee at the Greek corner of the huge metropolis.

In Astoria there are, besides the Cathedral of Agia Triada (Holy Trinity), two or three smaller Greek orthodox churches which we always pass during our stroll. Every time we find ourselves before a church, something like a magnet softly attracts my soul to its interior.

As we walk around with not a care in the world, we meet two more friends. We laugh and tease one another openly, but seeing the small orthodox church I feel this exciting attraction. I go in easily, with no warning to the rest of the group, saying:

"Guys, a Greek church! I'm going in to light a candle."

The rest follow me with the same motions. I walk up to the church altarpiece, bow before the icon of Christ and then before the icon of the Virgin. In front of it I have an unprecedented feeling of inner jubilation which covers my whole being like an armor. It cannot be described with words. No matter how hard I try, it cannot be described.

I have no time to say a prayer. I am overwhelmed with emotions and tears start flowing down my face uncontrollably. As I'm looking at the Virgin's eyes, I have the feeling she is alive as if she wants to tell me something.

My friends look at me in astonishment, as I am trying to wipe away the tears, embarrassed, while my eyes are still fixed on the icon of the Virgin.

"What is the matter, Peter?"

"Forgive me… I remembered something related to Greece and became emotional."

I felt ashamed. I was in a difficult position for having suddenly started to cry, but I had to say something to excuse myself.

We continue our walk through Manhattan and we do some window shopping, but I am not there, mentally. I couldn't shake what had just happened to me.

"Forgive me, guys, I'm going home. I suddenly have a very bad headache."

"We will accompany you home. You're looking pale."

"No, don't worry. I'm fine. I just want to walk and take in some fresh air. We'll talk over the phone later."

I walk for about an hour and a half. A large distance to cover on foot, but I really need it. When I finally arrive home, I feel incredibly exhausted and have to lie down; I do not even have the strength to take off my clothes. It is 6.00 in the afternoon and I soon fall asleep. I sleep until the following morning.

It is Sunday. We have arranged to meet with the whole group to walk around the fanciful streets in the center of Manhattan. As we walk, I see a sign: "Fortune Teller $5."

"Guys, what do you think? Shall we go and have our fortune read? It will be fun, right?"

"Konstantina, are you curious to find out if they know your future?"

"Are we really going to waste our money on this?"

"Come on, it'll be fun."

"I, as Peter, know my future. I will have a career as a singer."

"Come on! Either we all go or nobody goes" insists Konstantina.

The "shop" is in a basement. We start going down some steps and enter a dark room. At the back, there is a long, barely visible sofa behind which a figure is moving.

Suddenly, I'm feeling afraid and I start to sweat. We approach with small steps and see a dark-skinned woman of age with all-white afro hair, without any doubt a Gypsy.

"Welcome" she says. "There are five of you. I will call you one by one to come in to the small room."

One by one my friends go in and I try to hear what she is saying. Everything she tells them has a happy ending – that is, she tells them exactly what they want to hear to find relief.

Then it's my turn, but the Gypsy calls on Konstantina, who is behind me, to come in first.

"You will stay there and come in last" she tells me.

After a while, I see Konstantina come out of the room and go up the steps.

"Peter, I will wait for you out on the street."

Before I have time to move on, I see the Gypsy come out of the little room and come towards me. *Strange things are happening,* I think. *Instead of me going to the little room, she comes to me.*

She looks at me carefully, her eyes shining. She addresses me intensely with a stern voice.

"You will take a pumpkin and a candle, you will burn it entirely in front of the icon of the Virgin and whatever you ask of her, she will give to you."

Immediately, the words my mother had said when I was leaving my home for America come to mind. I am speechless because of what I have heard. I do not respond.

"Let me pay you."

"I want no money, my boy. Go in God's name. Follow the instructions I gave you."

I go slowly up the steps to meet my friends. I confess I did not expect to hear such words by a Gypsy in a Manhattan basement. I really do not know what just happened in the depth of my heart, my conscience and generally my whole existence.

I return to my apartment and immediately light a candle before the icon of the Virgin given to me by my mother. I refused to take the pumpkin as I could not understand how it was relevant.

I have no idea what to ask of the Virgin as I don't really know what I want in life. I stand before the icon for a long time, as the candle is burning, and ask the Virgin that her will be done in my life. I absolutely believe that, in the end, she will show me the way.

In spite of my good course of life, I feel a spiritual void inside me and a guilt for ungratefulness towards God. I feel that I am a sinner who struggles with passions. You might ask "well, who isn't?" As much as passions and temptations scare us, they humble us just as much.

How is a person to be humbled? We are so arrogant that the hammer of sin needs to hit us for us to ask for help, to humble ourselves. Sins provide life with experience and turn us to puzzlement. They help us to recognize ourselves and our weaknesses. We have to understand that we live life together with our passions. Passion is a dark symptom of human care, agony, stress and egoism. Often, seeing that we are struggling with our passions and do not defeat them, we get disappointed and continue to serve them. Before the temptations we are conquered by a tragic cowardice. We all have passions. The issue is how we manage and control them, so that they do not disorient us. At the same time, passion is great. It shows fortitude and a will to live. Those who struggle with passions are the ones who most appreciate life and serve its virtue.

Wednesday 15 March, 1978
Manhattan, New York

The years go by without care. I am now familiar with the world's metropolis; I am fully adapted to it and speak English fluently.

This week, some companies are visiting the university to carry out interviews with graduants in order to cover vacancies. It is a widely implemented tactic. In this way, companies recruit the best from each school, so that in the long run they form officials adapted to the corporate profile and culture.

I have realized that in this country you do not need to have a famous father or carry a history. Here, you create your own history. There is meritocracy, and it is no coincidence that the best brains in the world gather here.

Let us claim new time for our life.
Borrowed life is limited by restrictions imposed on it by others.
We need our own life, not a borrowed one.

As a senior student, something inside me pushes me to apply for an interview with companies related to my specialization in mechanical engineering. However, negative energy stops me from participating. I am afraid that my origin or even my accent are limiting factors in my selection.

But no, my fear will not prevail.

A life lived in fear is not a life.

In the end, I apply for participation only for the sake of the interview experience. I am thinking that one way or another I will go back to Greece after my post-graduate studies. I fill in the application of the interview. I have nothing to lose by going to three interviews with large corporations for an engineering position. It is an experience and at the same time my first contact with real economy.

Thursday 13 April, 1978
Campus

Today I have three consecutive interviews, one every half hour. I arrive at the university incredibly stressed. Every new and unknown thing causes us fear, but it must not break us. When we feel fear, we need to expand our comfort zone, in order to take a small step that may prove to be huge. Nobody knows until they take that step.

I feel like the interviews went quite well and I am anxiously awaiting the results. After a few days, on the central bulletin board of the university, the results are announced by the companies.

Two out of the three companies have announced their intention to employ me as project engineer. I cannot describe my joy, which is almost immediately replaced by a dilemma. One company proposes a job in Missouri, which is quite far away from my place of residence, while the second one quite close by, in New Jersey. I personally have no wish to leave New York, nor my friends from university. We have been through beautiful times together and have grown close. Besides, I love Manhattan. Why go to Missouri? I prefer living in the chaotic and fast rhythms of New York, the world metropolis.

I return home from the university on foot. It is a rainy day and I am walking through the streets of Manhattan. I hear the sound of rain, but also the sirens from ambulances and fire engines – customary sounds in New York. The famous yellow cabs pass by me. Momentarily I consider taking one, but I want to use this time to process the dilemma in my mind. People run to avoid getting wet, while I am walking without any care, as though my mind and body had been left to my next step. At some point the rain becomes stronger and the big imposing buildings cannot hold the force of the water. Still, I do not stop walking, although I am soaked through and through.

I finally arrive at the apartment. In the past twenty minutes I have made my decision: I will choose the company ICI Americas in Bayonne, New Jersey, almost one and a half hour from my apartment. The responsibilities of the position are the same in both companies, the annual income almost the same, so the dilemma is smaller. I will take a small risk, but also the commitment. Both are inseparable elements of my development.

I have read that some students were once called to participate in a study. One afternoon the first group of students was called to the university and they were encouraged to sign that they accepted to remain in the auditorium and take part in a working meeting, which they were later told would start at 07.00 am. They could, of course, be released if they wanted to with no consequences, as it was understandable that the time was somewhat discouraging. Almost 100% of the students remained for the meeting.

In the second group, students were informed at the start, before signing their participation, that the working meeting would start at 07.00 am. The result was that only 24% of the students remained for the meeting.

The reason I am mentioning this specific study is to show that every decision we make, if it is to be effective, presupposes commitment.

Commitment brings consistence.

Tuesday 23 May, 1978, Bayonne, New Jersey
ICI Americas Offices, a chemical company

Today I have a meeting with the personnel director about my employment at the company, straight after I graduate. I am waiting in the waiting room.

I am impressed. New offices, and this is the first time I am officially in a working environment related with the subject of my studies. It is also the first time I am wearing a suit in my life.

The personnel director informed me that they need me immediately and would want me to start the first week after my graduation.

"Could I please start in September instead of June? I have not been home to Greece in four years and I would like to spend a few days with my family."

"I understand. It is difficult to be far from your family for so many years. The most important thing in our life is our family and we need to keep tight and steady bonds with them. All right, you can start in September, but you must know that we will be very demanding, as we are with everybody."

"I thank you very much. I am ready for hard work, discipline and acquisition of new skills and knowledge."

I am entering one of the most important periods of my life, a period when psychology and morals are of high importance to me. I feel strong. I am officially an engineer, financially independent and with prospects that will – I hope – allow me to fulfill every one of my goals. I am in a country that generously provides you with opportunities, so long as you are willing to take them and work hard in order to achieve your goals.

First, effort is needed, then the way will follow.

Hard work! But we people like it easy and fast. But this combination is easily torn down. It lacks a strong foundation. Life requires insistence, patience, devotion and spiritual intuitions.

Saturday 3 June, 1978
Athens, Ellinikon, Eastern Airport

I am landing in Athens! The entire family is waiting to welcome me. My parents' and siblings' joy cannot be described. I cannot believe I am back home and cannot get enough of their embrace. I do not want to let them go. I have missed them so much!

We meet again after four years. I also see Spyros, my brother, with whom I have shared my first moments and anxieties in New York. He is now back in Greece working as an economist.

My parents have countless questions. On the one hand I want to see them and spend as much time with them as possible, but on the other I want to get lost in the Greek islands. I have missed Greece so much! Its light is dazzling and the blue in the sky the clearest in the color palette.

I have planned to start by visiting Ios, Santorini, Paros… and then we will see. Who knows what the rest of the summer has in store for me?

At the end of June, with no care in the world, I am in Santorini having a great time. The hotel receptionist tells me that my father called me. I return the call as soon as I get the chance.

"My son, I want you to visit the Holy Mount and in particular father Antonios, to tell him about my penitence and inform him that because of my health I will not be able to visit him as promised. I want you to go in my place, to get his blessing for success in your new job in the distant country."

"Father, I am on holiday, I want to enjoy the sun and the sea. I need to spend time with my friends. Understand me. We had no contact during all these years and I want to maintain the connection."

Friendship is a great thing, especially friendship with common experiences. It remains etched in your soul, and that is why, even if you lose touch with a friend, the shared experiences always follow you.

"Please, son, take a break to go to the Holy Mount and then you can continue your travels."

"All right, father. I cannot refuse."

Thursday 13 July, 1978
Athens

I am going to the Holy Mount for the first time and I am curious to see it. We start at the crack of dawn with my good friend Yannis, by car from Athens to Ouranoupolis which is on the third "leg" of Khalkidhiki. The trip takes several hours with frequent stops.

Ouranoupolis, entrance gate to the Holy Mount

We arrive around noon and ask some locals what time the next boat leaves for the Holy Mount.

"There is no boat. There is only one boat trip a day and it leaves at nine in the morning. You missed it. You'll have another chance tomorrow," they inform us.

We cannot waste an entire day, because we have to be back in Athens on Sunday night. On the beach, a little further on, we meet a fisherman tending to his nets.

"Good afternoon. We want to go to the Holy Mount and were told that we missed the boat. We have to enter the monastery today."

"Do you have permits?"

"We do not know the exact procedure. We are coming from Athens and had no time to get information. We just arrived."

"Since you have no permits, I cannot take you."

"We can reward you handsomely."

"Where exactly do you want to go?"

"To the Holy Monastery of Konstamonitou."

"Because you are young kids and are here for the first time, go to the edge at the end of the pier and I will come and get you in five minutes."

At the time it was allowed. Now something like that would be impossible.

Carrying our stuff, we get on the small boat at the pier of Ouranoupolis. We are the only pilgrims at that time. Everybody has left. There is dead silence in the village.

Entry to the Holy Mount is only possible by sea. We turn our eyes to the mountain and see the border separating the Holy Mount from the rest of the land of the third leg of Khalkidhiki. Enchanting nature spreads out before our very eyes. The natural beauty around you seems untouched by humanity. The first kellia appear before us, small houses usually housing a small group of monks whose activities – besides the religious ones – include agricultural work, handicraft, etc.

We have left the noise of the capital behind us. Our only company are the seagulls flapping their wings on both sides of our boat.

Going deeper into the Holy Mount you really feel something special; a different energy, peace. As if time no longer exists and you no longer care about what is happening in the outside world.

Eventually, one monastery after another begins to appear along the peninsula. The view is exquisite! The monasteries resemble byzantine castles, each with its own tower, stone walls all around and in between appear church domes of various sizes.

Unconsciously, a question forms inside you. How is it possible that we have such a live byzantine masterpiece in our country, like a museum, and not know it as Greeks?

The time came for us to disembark from the small boat in the shipyard[1] of the monastery. We have to walk for an hour

---

[1] The shipyards are small harbors where the boats of each monastery are kept and maintained.

and a half, all uphill. Alone, with our backpacks on our back, we start the ascent. After fifteen minutes, we enter a beautiful forest which offers us breaths of coolness in high summer. In the mist, we watch the monastery from afar, which looks like a stone castle, invincible, byzantine.

After a steep ascent, we arrive at the monastery. We were not expected and so there is nobody to receive us. Right outside the main gate of the monastery, to the left, we see an old monk, over seventy years old, moving around kneeling on one leg in a small garden tending to the flowers one by one.

We had been told that each time we met a monk on our way, we should say "Bless," the customary monastic greeting.

"Bless" we tell him, as we walk beside him to enter in the main monastery.

"The Lord. Welcome, boys. Where do you come from?"

"From Athens, father."

"Go in, go to the Archontariki (guest house) to your right as you go in, in the pilgrim reception area."

We pass a huge wooden gate, the entrance of the monastery, which closes at sunset. Exactly in front of us to the left there is an imposing church, the katholikon of the monastery (conventual church). Around it there are very old two-story buildings, in Macedonian architecture, with broad balconies and rooms on the left and right. We are speechless.

We are met by the archontaris, the monk in charge of hospitality.

"Shall we offer you the traditional treat of the Holy Mount? Raki to stop the hiker's sweat, loukoum to get a sweet taste and help him to quickly recover his strength thanks to the sugars it contains, water to still his thirst and coffee to invigorate him."

We enjoy the treat and get a first taste of the hospitality on the Holy Mount. Then the archontaris leads us to a huge room with ten camp beds. Luckily, we are the only pilgrims that day.

"Father, please, may I meet father Antonios?"

"Peter, the father is ill and will not be able to see you today. Tomorrow, if he is feeling better, he will receive you in his cell."

"Please, can you inform him that my father sent me to meet him?"

"Tomorrow we will talk again, do not worry. Have a good rest."

Everything around us is unique and unprecedented, from the interior decoration, the 1821 heroes hanging on the walls, to the immense silence, the peaceful and solemn atmosphere emanating from this blessed place.

We retire early to our room, after the informal "lights out" at sundown. Nothing moves after sunset; there is absolute silence. Tired from the trip, we have no problem falling asleep so early.

Five and a half hours have passed when, at around two in the morning, a monk knocks on our door rather strongly.

"Guys, get up! The mass has started."

We look at each other in surprise. We have no choice and get up immediately. The room is dark and we can hardly find our clothes to get dressed. The only burning oil lamps are in the corridor outside our room and in the common toilets. There is no electricity. For heating there are wood stoves everywhere and cooking is done exclusively with wood.

With great difficulty we walk down the steps leading to the katholikon, the main church of the monastery, among four other chapels, built at the four corners of the building complex. The only thing you see are black robes moving in the dark.

We can hardly make out the entrance to enter the church. The view and the atmosphere are incredibly reverential. Oil lamps are hanging with humble lighting and almost all pews right and left are filled with monks, most of them of age. There are some young ones, too, however. They are each holding a long set of prayer beads which they are turning with their fingers. Each knot is a prayer, as they call the phrase "Lord Jesus Christ, have mercy on me."

After bowing, we begin to feel embarrassed as we do not know what to do. A tall, imposing monk approaches us and waves for us to come in further. We go on timidly and, after crossing a space called liti (internat narthex), we enter the main church.

The church is built in the byzantine style with a cross-in-square shape. On the right and left there are the cantors' choruses in semi-circular shape and in the middle of each half-circle there is a music stand. Exactly in the middle of the main church, a huge bronze chandelier is hanging from the dome and two-headed eagles are around, with representations of saints and apostles in between. The church in dedicated to St. Stephanos.

At this point I would like to tell you, for history's sake, that after the millennial celebrations of the Holy Mount in 1963, everybody said that it would be its end. Only old men were left, as after the war no young people came anymore, as had been the case during the war as well. The end of the 1970s was a transitional period for the Holy Mount. After the decline of past decades due to the First and Second World Wars, the Holy Mount started to flourish with the arrival of new monks, even educated ones, who started slowly staffing the various monasteries, the result being that today all holy monasteries have become coenobitic[2] instead of idiorrhythmic[3] and so we now have a flourishing Holy Mount with almost two thousand monks.

Five hours later, mass is over. We walk towards the exit of the church at about seven in the morning. We follow the monks and end up in a big dining room, prepared for everyone, monks and guests. This is the main hall, called trapeza (refectory), where they have their meal after mass has ended. The main meal of the day is served first thing in the morning. In the evening, after evensong, dinner is served, which is a simple and optional meal.

We enter a huge imposing hall with wooden monastic tables, each with space for ten pilgrims. The monk responsible for the meal shows us where to sit. I am astonished looking at the murals around the room. In the back, the abbot's table and behind it sits the elders' assembly (gerontia[4]), usually consisting of six to eight monks, depending on the monastery. All the monks sit together and in the next tables are reserved for the pilgrims or lay people – as they call us.

---

[2] These monasteries have a daily unified program and everything is communal.

[3] Monasteries where monks live independent of one another, without common program, except on Sundays.

[4] The administrative body of the monastery.

The meal today includes a satisfying serving of cooked green beans, a salad with cucumber, tomato and lots of onion, and one apple each. In the middle of the table there is a small basket with hand-made bread and a metal platter with olives for everyone. A simple yet tasty, healthy and satiating meal.

As soon as we start eating, one monk – the reader – reads the story of the saint celebrated today. I have surrendered to the experience of the moment. What I see is forever recorded on my soul's hard drive. Such moments are brought up from memory when we really need them, to give us strength. They resound on the emotional field and are automatically activated whenever we experience deep stimulations.

The glasses we drink our water from are made of tin, as are the plates. There is no luxury. Seated as I am, I am watching everything around me – icons, objects, faces. I feel lost. A pilgrim sitting next to me realized it and said: "Whoever comes once to the Holy Mount, comes again. The place draws you; it brings you back."

During the meal it is strictly forbidden to talk, so I just nodded affirmatively. The meal only lasts for ten to fifteen minutes and the procedure requires dedication and respect. After the meal, the abbot stands to bless the monks and pilgrims as they exit the refectory, while on the other side of him the cook, the monk responsible for the refectory and the reader are bowing, asking for forgiveness, in case they did something wrong in their respective fields of responsibility.

Going out, I realize that in the world we rarely ask our neighbors for forgiveness for a mistake or an omission we have committed, while here they ask for forgiveness beforehand, in case they feel they have committed a mistake. I was confronted with the concept of humility and started to see the "all important" ego in a more subservient role.

After the end of the meal, we meet the archontaris, who is waiting to take us to the father's cell. Daybreak is just starting. He knocks discreetly on his cell's door, opens it and beckons for us to enter.

"Father, the young men are here to receive your blessing."

He helps him get up from the bed, so that he may see us better.

I look at his face that lights up the whole cell around us like a light – which is no exaggeration. Seeing him, I am instantly overcome by a sense of delight and elation.

"Father, your blessing. My father is sending me from Athens. Because of his health he could not come himself, so I am transmitting his penitence."

I approach him in order to kiss his hand, and I hear him murmur in a trembling voice:

"You are the son of my Paul, the son of my Paul."

He puts his arms around me. My head touches his chest. Suddenly, I feel an aura rising from his womb, also felt by Yannis. We sit exactly opposite him. He is holding in his callused hand a set of prayer beads with big knots, worn out from long-lasting use. In that moment, I feel a strong sense of gratitude for being alive at this moment. Spiritually uneducated, I do not know what to ask him. I'm a bit lost and my gestures betray embarrassment as well as a lack of experience.

The archontaris warns us that we must leave, as the father's health is poor.

As we are ready to leave, I suddenly get over my shyness, I embrace him, kiss his hand, tears fill my eyes and I ask him to pray for me and, especially, for the new course I am about to take in America as a mechanical engineer.

He bends down and whispers into my ear: "Son, you must say the prayer. The prayer must become your breath."

"Father, I do not know the prayer."

"Lord Jesus Christ, have mercy on me."

I ask him if we can take a picture and he allows it. I have since framed it and hung it on the wall in the cell I now live in. I kiss it every day. But the biggest blessing the father left me is that worn out set of prayer beads, which the archontaris kept and delivered to me after he passed at the age of ninety-six. It is a pilgrimage that is etched very deeply into my heart. All the things we saw and the few words we exchanged were enough to redetermine my inner being and to initiate me to another perspective and dimension of life, which had never crossed my mind, which made me wonder and be intensely concerned. Is it possible that our life is not so fleeting after all?

I wondered about human nature. I thought for a moment that it is no coincidence that the great Greek philosophers and tragic poets tried through their work to approach and define man. I concluded briefly the definition given by Socrates, i. e. that man is someone who considers and judges all he has seen, and if something distinguishes us as beings, as Aristotle used to say, it is our aptitude for knowledge.

Where do I want to go with all of this? We see, watch, examine and evaluate what is right in life. And that can only be achieved by developing knowledge. Man has the need to create, without weakening his imagination; to reproduce knowledge, but without abolishing its aspects that are unknown and hidden to him.

In the world we live in, we will never know everything,
we will never conquer perfection.

With all this in my mind, it is time for us to return.

I am standing alone looking at the sea. This place is free from temptation and distractions. The land untouched by time. Its limited accessibility provides it a freedom to breathe. The bigger the breath, the deeper you immerse yourself in spiritual freedom. You see beauty with different eyes. The more you surrender yourself to the Mount, the bigger your internal cleansing will be. A holy place, of unadulterated purity and incessant flow of spiritual energy.

Man must see an horizon instead of fog
in whatever he does in his life.

We start the trip back to Athens. Throughout the entire journey we talk about the Holy Mount. It is impossible for the images, experiences, the whole event, to leave our mind, even for a second.

And after my return to Athens, I am still questioning my priorities in life. Before leaving for New York, my sister and my father persuade me to visit father Porfyrios (he is now a saint), although I personally wanted to avoid it.

The father lives alone in a shack in Oropos, Attica. He opens the door before we even had time to knock. He sees us and addresses me personally.

"Peter, my son, welcome!." He embraces and kisses me. "Come in, my son, let's talk. I want to tell you about my plans for the future. Here in the back, we will build a big women's monastery. Can you please look for some insulating material to place between the walls?"

I had not mentioned anything regarding my studies and the work I would start in America, yet he starts analyzing technical issues with such detail, as though he were describing my new job accurately. He talks to me about energy exploitation of the gas emitted as flame by refineries and I start to ask myself about this impressive coincidence of the subject matter. *He is either a saint or simply misguided.*

"Come, let's go outside now, the others are waiting," he tells me.

"Father, I want your advice on a personal matter puzzling me. Can I share it with you?"

"Better leave it. Don't continue, because you will suffer."

"Father, let me tell you what is happening."

"Leave it, son. You will have problems."

Creation goes through desire, claim, visualization.

The wonderful summer in Greece is ending. I say goodbye to parents, brothers and sisters and close friends and return to America. My feelings are mixed, but the future will tell.

Tuesday 29 May, 1979

ICI Americas company, Bayonne, New Jersey

A new start, new dreams, new motivation. I adapt easily to the now day-to-day.

Although I am new at the job, I am doing well enough and am keen to learn and advance. I am also conceited; I cannot hide it. I wish to have a great career; to be at the top of the world. The principles I grew up by also define my professional attitude and my superiors recognize it. In fact, they do not hesitate to show me their satisfaction with my proficiency and quick adjustment to the needs and requirements of the company.

It is not enough to have an innate inclination or talent.
It gets lost easily if you do not cultivate your skills
and do not work hard,
With eagerness, passion, and self-denial.

"Peter, please come into my office for a moment."

"In five minutes, Chris. I have to send a report."

"Peter, as a company, we consider it important – for reasons related to the development of our officials – to reward the efforts of our employees. So, we evaluated the application you filed for financing the post-graduate studies you wish to attend in techno-economics at New York University and, together with management, we have decided to wholly finance the cost of your studies."

"First of all, I want to thank you, but I would like to know, if you can tell me, how my application was selected."

"Our criteria are purely meritocratic. We want our partners to develop, because, with them, the company will develop. The company is not an abstract notion; it is its people. If officials do not progress, the business doesn't either. The greatest capital of a company is its personnel and building this immaterial asset is based on development. Development has principles and rules and that is why companies prefer people with values, who can support their own growth and, in passing this on, help the development of the company.

At the same time, let us not forget that the orientation of the company is focused on giving. Its establishment and operation have no meaning if it does not also give back to society. And on that level of social utility, every employee of the company must feel like an integral part of this process of giving.

At this point, allow me to analyze the concept of giving on a human level. Giving has four levels. The first: I am giving from what I have, I share my belongings, but I keep something for me. The second: I give everything I have; I give it all, I am left with nothing but myself. The third: I give from what I am, from myself, from my existence, I spend myself. And finally: I give what I am, I offer my whole self, without holding back, without remainders; I am left with nothing, not even myself, I become vacant.

We strive, we seek to give from what we have and what we are and, if possible, give our heart wholly. The highest condition of all is to sympathize, ache together, not in the sense of suffering, but in the sense of consubstantiation, i.e.

experience the other's problem as our own, wholly participate, carry his burden, which in essence serves as a personal awakening.

At the company, Peter, we try to instill in our employees this mindset. Because tomorrow it may be us who will need help. There must always be someone willing to extend a helping hand. If we do not cultivate sympathy, we have failed as a species."

"Chris, I recognize that what you are conveying is important and I totally identify with the values of the company. Thank you for this opportunity. I promise to repay your trust through hard work and by giving back to the company, to society and my fellow men."

I decide to start my post-graduate studies in Technical Economics at the University of New York. I want to acquire further knowledge, as it will assist me in my future endeavors. We must possess general education and skills in order to be able to respond with balanced success and dignity to the requirements of society. The challenges are many and continue to grow. We therefore need flexibility and a continuous expansion of our knowledge.

One year later, New York

I am living the freest period of my life. At twenty-three I am roaming in New York. My friendship with my former University colleagues, especially those who followed the same path as I, has not only survived, but is getting stronger and stronger.

It is a time without obligations and limitations. I very much love sports; I work out every day and love watching all the different sports teams. My favorite team in basketball is the New York Nicks and I try not to miss a game. I also love hockey and the New York Rangers and often attend their matches. But, most of all, I love baseball and the New York Yankees. I admire Reggie Jackson, an excellent player with great talent. Sport is a fountain of life. It changes your mind, improves you, and makes you discover your limits.

All this time, however, it is impossible to extinguish the Greek fire inside me. There is no New York without Astoria. In my free time I often visit the Greek shops, as well as the Greek restaurants Hestia and Philoxenia in Manhattan, and Kalyva or Spilia in Astoria, to enjoy the tastes reminding me of my mother's, but also to reminisce about home. How I miss the smells of Greek cooking!

Studio 54, the most famous disco-club of the world
54th Street, Upper East Side, Manhattan

I am particularly fond of Manhattan's Upper East Side and in the evening, we often visit with my friends at the famous night club, Studio 54. It was the first place to introduce face control at the entrance.

It was very difficult, sometimes even impossible, to get in. Even as a member, if the bouncer didn't like you, there was no way for you to get in. And the selection was rigorous and incomprehensible. "You get in. You don't, I don't like the way you look." As simple as that! "Go wash yourselves," was a phrase that was often heard as well, with no sign of discretion or shame.

Eccentricity and glamour at the same time. It operated for only thirty months, from 1977 until 1981. History has recorded it as a legendary night club in a colorful and intense era, with authentic stars. Hundreds of people waited in line for hours every night, trying to ignore the brutal New York cold and almost never managing to pass the gates of entertainment "heaven," where everything was allowed. Among the famous guests were many Greeks, too. Christina Onassis had been photographed dancing on the dance floor, surrendered to the carefree rhythms of the music and so was Vicky Leandros, but also Philip Niarchos.

The typical feature of the club was a huge moon in the shape of a human face, hanging over the dance floor, among dancers' cages. A huge automatic spoon would approach the face and feed it, at which point the moon would light up. The contents of the spoon would change depending on the party and the substances being served. The atmosphere was always charged. In the basement, there were mattresses strewn around and drugs circulated freely. A legendary club that made its name as an adult playground.

The whole of New York's elite and "subculture" considered it their base camp. You could dance and watch Andy Warhol, Calvin Klein, Elisabeth Taylor, Mick Jagger, John Travolta, Michael Jackson, Tina Turner, Diana Ross, Sher, Salvador Dali, get drunk on cocktails. There has even been a film made about Studio 54 and thousands of articles have been written about this one-of-a-kind club all round the world. Some articles mention that there is a philosophy behind all of this, summarized in one phrase: "The key to a good party is to fill a room with guests who are more interesting than you."

At the door some millionaires try to get in, flagrantly boasting about their financial status, in an attempt to have better luck at the entrance. "I am a millionaire and I want to spend money."

"If they're not fun and don't come to have a good time, I don't care who they are," one of the owners told us. Perhaps this was the secret to the success of the club.

"Here, you come to have fun. If you came because of your ego, go someplace else," you often heard them say at the door. "We want everybody to be beautiful, well dressed and in the mood to enjoy themselves."

Customers – common people, models, popular clubbers, sportspeople – all enjoy themselves frenetically, with the help of drinks and drugs. One evening, we approach the entrance and we see one of the two owners, Steve Rubell, suddenly come out and look at the people.

"You and you, come in," he said to two men with moustaches, wearing a dress and a skirt respectively. "You need better clothes to enter here," he continued, addressing a young woman. "You, on my right. Yes, you, looking at me; get in the taxi over there, go home and change and come back and perhaps you will make it. You two, why don't you go elsewhere to have a drink? Here you will wait for several days before entering. You may even never get in."

Almost a hundred people have gathered outside, pleading to get in the club, with their fingers raised like little children, for the doormen to see them. Hazing, irony and arrogance are part of the legend they try to maintain in every way.

Luckily, we found the way for the doormen to recognize me. We take care to always be well dressed, in order to be allowed to go in and enjoy ourselves freely and with no obstacles, no limits. As soon as they see us, they beckon for us come forward.

"Welcome, Greek guys! Opa!"

They adore Greece, and this is our passport to enter.

You go in and sit in the comfortable red armchairs, with pillows at the back that can be adjusted in various positions. If you want, you can lie down and wait for the waitress to come for you to choose your cocktail, while watching the dancers sway to the rhythm of the music.

I am also sitting in a spacious leather armchair and I see Bob Dylan relaxing in the next one. We start talking. A truly polite man. Another famous person loving our country and our culture.

I say goodbye to him and we enter the next room. There is a huge 3-dimensional screen showing animals fighting for survival and arrows flying directly at you; people who've had too many drinks duck to avoid them!

Before me I see a guy in a t-shirt saying "Fuck Studio 54." The owner approaches him and tells him he will have free entrance, whenever he wants. Paranoia at its highest! The club may project this image of having a strict door policy, but inside, those responsible wish to have harmonious co-existence and cooperation between employees and customers. Waiters are perhaps the most valuable employees. They are first-line employees.

But the lights and sound are also all perfect. It is obvious that details are important to them and they leave nothing to chance. Everything functions with mathematical accuracy, because everything is equally important and balance and moderation must be maintained.

We are in an "atmospheric" space, where waiters must, while working, also entertain and dance. It is the owners' strategy. They encourage employees to be friendly, have a good time themselves and be very relaxed. All the people inside the club must have a good time and forget their problems. Clever instructions which are definitely effective.

The crowd enjoying itself resembles a multi-colored beehive. Here people come to forget their troubles and not bother about anything. The doors to private rooms and suites open and close and "figures" go in and out to satisfy their carnal instincts. The ultimate freedom! Everything works with mutual respect. Despite the guests' varying characters, you see before you a seriousness, in particular in their gestures and attitude; it's impressive to see. There are rules of politeness and good behavior. There is no intention to offend. They all know the reason why they are there.

People live coveting rather than tasting pleasure

One night, a group of Harvard students came in. As soon as they appeared in their expensive suits and ties, they were let in. For the next couple of hours, the only people passing the door of the disco were transsexuals who, according to the owners, could be terrific company for the Harvard boys.

Andy Warhol, a daily guest of the club, said: "At the door there was a dictatorship, but in the club, there was absolute democracy."

Three years later

32nd Street, between Maddison and 5th Avenue

After four years of hard work and having finished my post-graduate studies, I decide to apply for a position at a larger company in order to better utilize the knowledge I have acquired with my post-graduate degree.

One morning, I receive an unexpected phone call from a recruitment agency. They inform me about a vacancy in one of the top companies of the world. I answer that I have no reason to leave my company at that particular time, that I am totally satisfied with my current position and have plenty of prospects. They tell me that they are looking for a project engineer and that the job will offer an enticing salary. Finally, I decide to go to the interview, just for the experience. You never know where life may lead you… I feel I am standing well on my own feet.

*

I see a student wishing to intervene.

"Yes, we are listening."

"Father, I am listening to your story very carefully and I would like to ask you how you interpret the terms of good and bad luck. And a second question, if I may. Regarding adventurism, do you believe it is necessarily a negatively charged concept? Thank you."

"Good and bad luck differ only by a word. Bad luck is often attributed to bad conditions, bad coincidences, other people and sometimes our misfortune. On the other hand, good luck is attributed to our capabilities, our courage, our audacity, sometimes fortune itself. The line separating good from bad luck is very thin. Good luck is associated with faith in the result, the purpose, ourselves, while bad luck is respectively associated with low self-esteem, procrastination, a lack of goals. He who dares usually has good luck, while he who does nothing has bad luck. Luck smiles at us, when we try continuously. The greater the effort, the better the luck.

Some people were born in environments where conditions provided more opportunities for advancement, with better conditions regarding personal self-fulfillment and bliss compared to others. Still, a significant proportion of these people did not manage to be "lucky." The reason lies in the way they managed and used these opportunities. If our choices do not produce the required results, we easily call them "bad luck." It would be good, therefore, to see ourselves and imagine us in the future, to be careful how we interpret events and constantly verify them, avoiding frivolous interpretations. The most important thing of all, however, is to be focused on our goals, developing each time the possibility to adapt them. Briefly, we should be receptive to our personal "luck." Luck is for each one of us a personal calling.

Now, regarding adventurism, the adventurer is conquered by passions and his devotion to the achievement of his goals motivates the negative sign of the skills and strengths he may have. An adventurer is someone who sides up with his personal and intrinsic tendency to win and achieve his personal goal by unfair ways and attitudes. But this is in contrast with common good and operational result, which he himself may benefit from and enjoy, but it will always be at the expense of other fellow humans.

So, on the face of it, we are looking at a person who indeed seems successful, but essentially, from a moral point of view, is in decline."

Christmas – New Year's Eve, 1984
New York – Jamaica

Heavy winter. In the morning we rid our cars of the snow from the previous evening. Temperatures are in free fall, reaching well below zero. At one point I saw the temperature in the car fall to -32 degrees Celsius. I feel cold just by thinking back on it. An enchanting image, seeing the lights in Times Square covered in snowflakes.

Everybody is preparing for the New Year's festivities. The shop windows are decorated, competing amongst each other in originality and trying their utmost to pull any prospective customers in. Some brave people are out on the streets, holding a hot beverage to keep warm. There's a festive atmosphere all around.

The idea to go to a warmer climate to celebrate New Year's soon entered my mind. Our options for a festive escape within the USA were numerous, but me and my friends preferred the Caribbean. Naturally, Jamaica came to mind, that island with the impressive palm trees and endless blue-green beaches. From freezing cold to sweltering heat in the heart of winter. Our love for reggae music and Bob Marley definitely is another reason for us to visit Jamaica.

We undertake a little research to find the best holiday package. We will have seven whole days of travel and relaxation at our disposal. We can't wait!

Finally, on 26th December, we take off from JFK airport for the Caribbean paradise, with a two-hour stopover in

Florida. We kill time with the electronic games at the airport, until we run out of coins.

During the hour and a half flight to our final destination, I am glued to the airplane window, looking at the dot-islands of the Caribbean. We land at the airport of Kingston, the capital of Jamaica. As I walk to the airplane exit, a wave of warm air washes over me. I immediately take off the cardigan I was wearing, tie it around my waist and feel the change of climate.

While we are waiting for our suitcases, I see a thermometer showing 37 degrees Celsius, and it is still only 1.00 pm. We go out and look for a taxi to take us to the hotel. In the typical relaxed attitude, an African American approaches and asks us:

"Do you want a taxi? Where are you going?"

"To the Montego Bay hotel."

"Wait here. I am coming in a yellow car. I will carry your luggage."

A moment later, he appears in his car. "Get in" he says.

"Thanks, boss!"

"Where are you coming from?"

"New York."

"Cold! How can you live there in such hectic rhythms? Come here to live in the land of relaxation."

"Our jobs are in New York. We cannot leave them."

"You will always be busy and you will always look for something better, something more, and you will always miss something. There is no end to this. To relax, I will offer you first-quality grass from my garden. Let's go cut it now. It is well worth a detour and a stop. It is fresh and home-made. Just to welcome you in Jamaica."

Some time later, we arrive at a wonderful spot, in Montego Bay, where we will spend the next seven days. Our hotel is right next to the sea, and palm trees are so close, that you think they are watered by the sea. We do not miss the opportunity and put on our swimming trunks and head directly for the beach. White sand with gold speckles and blue crystal-clear water with palm trees reflected on the surface. We are warned not to swim outside the red buoys, as there is the risk of meeting a shark.

The feel of the water is unique. The scenery is wonderful; it makes you forget the rhythms and the stress of New York. As you swim, you see small harmless sharks swimming alongside you. The momentary feeling of fear turns to enthusiasm within minutes.

> *In nature life co-exists harmoniously, but only if we humans respect its rules.*

The carefree days pass beautifully. We have the chance to dine in unique restaurants and enjoy outstanding local cuisine recipes. It is a very beautiful place, with kind people and interesting culture.

Monday 13th February, 1984
New Jersey, Company offices, 12.30 pm

I drive for an hour and a half from home and arrive at the Research and Development Center of the company. The man who will interview me is late. I am waiting patiently in the waiting room.

"Mr. Ioannidis, Mr. Andrew will be a little late. He is very sorry, but something unexpected came up. Would you like some coffee?"

"No, thank you. No problem, I will wait. Thanks for letting me know."

My heart is about to break, when half an hour later I am being interviewed by probably the biggest company of the 1980s.

"Mr. Ioannidis, I am sorry for the delay. I am Michael Andrew. Usually, I am very punctual for my appointments and careful with my time. It is time for lunch, shall we go to the company restaurant and talk there?"

"Thank you. With great pleasure."

"Your family name is not American, is it?" he says as soon as we sit down at a table.

"No, that's right. I'm Greek. I left when I was eighteen and studied at the University of New York. I have worked as a mechanical engineer ever since."

"I admire Greece. I had the chance to visit it once, but also to read about your great civilization. Tell me, why did you apply for this specific position?"

"My ambition is to work for a big company, acquire new working experience, and to learn and progress as a human being and a scientist."

"Mr. Ioannidis, let me tell you a few things about the company. At the moment we are the biggest chemical and petroleum product company in the world. We like to recruit people with dedication, who love the work, but who also like to have a laugh every now and then. We do not want miserly people. The company offers significant advancement opportunities and, moreover, production takes place through the transfer of knowledge. Allow me to tell you a story.

Once, a company invited an engineer to solve a technical problem with a machine due to an unexpected breakdown. The engineer spent three days studying the machine. On the fourth day he changes a specific screw and gives it different turns. The machine worked again. The next day, he sends the company an invoice for 10.000 dollars. The owner of the company sees it and the amount seems excessive to him. "If you explain the cost, I will pay it," he says. The engineer sends the analysis which states: Change and installation of the screw: $10. Exact identification of the screw that needed to change and the turns at which the machine must be screwed in order to function: $9.990. In other words,

knowledge has value, and here we recognize and reward it."

"Mr. Andrew, I am by nature a studious person and try to carry out every task assigned to me effectively, conscientiously and morally. I always work with discipline and respect for my colleagues."

"How do you address competition? Are you a competitive person?"

"Yes, I am competitive and my ambition is to reach a high hierarchical position."

"That is the kind of partner we're looking for, so that our employees motivate one another and, through competition, help the company advance."

After talking and eating for an hour and a half the interview is over. What I realized was that, through the interview process, Mr. Andrew tried to understand my character more than my knowledge. It is true that many companies now apply a more people-focused approach to their prospective officials. Subsequently, I read an article explaining that big companies mainly recruit characters.

Leaving the interview, I have a feeling that all went well. Later, I hear that they had already enquired about my professional experience. Recommendations often are a deciding factor for a working position. Who recommends us and what they say about us is incredibly important.

Seven days later

My beeper rings. It shows the phone number of the headquarters of the New Jersey giant. Immediately I look for a phone to call back. I am very anxious.

I am informed that they considered me the most suitable candidate for the position and am asked to come to their offices to sign my new contract as large-scale project engineer.

"Mr. Ioannidis, you will assume your new duties immediately."

"If possible, I would like to start in three weeks in order to inform my current employer of my resignation, so that they will have the time to employ someone new or promote a colleague to my position. In any case, I would not like to abandon them; it is unethical."

My start is like a dream. Like the dreams we have when something new starts, not necessarily caring what will happen in the future, but what we are experiencing in the present. Like the dreams we had as children about the future, but living intensely our every moment.

All goes smoothly, when one day my car breaks down. No harm done. It is a breakdown and will be fixed. But until it is fixed, I must find a way to return home.

In my team I have a foreman for a demanding project we are carrying out. He offered to drive me from New Jersey to Manhattan for three days, until I got the car back from the shop. We finish at about the same time, so it is convenient for both, and I would not get him off schedule.

On the third day we have finished and are ready to go.

"Peter, there is a problem. My partner will come home late today and I have no keys."

"No problem, Michael. Come to my apartment; we will sit together and have some whisky, waiting for her to come home."

32nd Street, between Maddison and 5th Avenue

We are in the living room. In front of us there is a glass table. While we are drinking our whisky, Michael takes a small bag of cocaine out of his pocket, he spreads the powder, breaks it and draws six lines. I am speechless.

"Come on, Peter, try some. Don't be shy."

"Thank you, Michael. I have never tried it and I don't want to."

He continues and sniffs twice more from each nostril. He is high. He is in high spirits. He tells jokes and I laugh in my embarrassment. I do not know how to deal with it. Then, he has six more sniffs.

"What are you doing?" I ask.

Before I even finish my sentence, he's already out of it. I am shocked and fear that he may lose conscience in my apartment and that I may be accused of possession and use of cocaine. I start slapping him and, in the end, I throw water at him. I cannot think of anything else.

He eventually comes round. I try to get him down to the parking area, where his car is. With difficulty, we make it down the stairs.

"Michael, are you serious? Are you going to drive? You know you can't."

"I am fine."

"Are you serious? You are in no position to drive."

"I told you, don't worry about me."

I am trying to prevent him from driving, but in vain. He's persistent. I am stunned, because he has never shown anything like this during work.

Shocked, I return to my apartment and am thinking of what will happen tomorrow at the office. Will he show up? And in what condition?

Next morning, he comes to the site in excellent state. He says he's sorry. One person during the day, another in the evening.

"Michael, what you do in your personal life is none of my business, but when it affects your work performance, we have a serious problem."

"I'm sorry, I overdid it."

"Apology accepted. However, beyond all else, your life is of course your own, but your behavior affects others as well."

We realize that we are on the right path, thanks to the quality of those who we invite into our life, because they have something to tell us, something to teach us.

Life is like a scale. When you feel something is burdening you, you must throw away inner weights in order to feel light and flexible, so that you can take a creative step.

We must take away mistakes and add hope.

If you focus on one thing, you disregard another area of your life, which may be more important than the one you place all of your attention and care on.

Life is true when you find your center,
when you feel well with yourself.

Balance in our life is a difficult equation, but not impossible to solve.

3 years later

The course is difficult but upwards. Time goes by fast and I continue my work with dedication and decisiveness. I like my job. I am productive and effective and am promoted to head technical manager of the company. I am now in charge of and will supervise all of our projects in the USA and abroad.

As the technical manager I am in direct contact with the president and CEO of the company. I report directly to him and my proposals are approved exclusively by him. The company president is of Armenian origin, he knows Greece, having visited it with his family, and has led me to understand that he has positively judged my character, my values and my effectiveness in decision-making, as well as my managerial competences. Perhaps he sees in me some leadership potential. I assume he does, because he often calls me into his office for my opinion on various important decisions. Perhaps he wants to evaluate my judgement in connection to my morals. A basic point of friction between us are sports, where sometimes we disagree.

Monday 3rd November 1987

New Jersey

"Mr. Ioannidis, the president wants to see you in his office."

"Tell him no ... I am joking, I'll be there in two minutes."

He will probably ask me about the difficulties and the delay we are having with one of our projects. I have already explained it to him.

"Can I come in?"

"I am glad to see you, Peter. Today is Tuesday and I would like to invite you over to my holiday home in Miami this coming extended weekend."

"Thank you for the invitation. You catch me unawares, but I really can't refuse your invitation."

I am excited for my trip to Indian Creek in Miami, the "billionaires' island," as they call it. It's an island with a number of high-security villas belonging to wealthy families.

It is Thursday today and I will leave the office early in order to take the afternoon flight to Miami. I arrive late and I am welcomed in their magnificent home by his wife and their daughter Colette, whom they affectionately call Coco. They wish me a good night's rest and we agree to meet in the morning, to have breakfast on the central balcony of the house which has an incredible view.

In the morning we have a relaxed conversation and completely forget that it's my boss sitting across from me. They are pleasant people with a good sense of humor. The discussion turns to Greece and they relate their experiences from their trip. They admire our culture, but there is another important link between us: religion. They are all Christians.

The other three daughters and their husbands soon join the company. entire as the only outsider.

Colette and I start spending time together and become close. There is chemistry between us and we have common interests. Our discussions are never-ending.

My three-day stay is over and I am getting ready to leave for the airport. I am overcome by a bitter-sweet taste. It is time to say goodbye and thank my hosts. Colette proposes to drive me to the airport.

We are attracted to one another and we make a new appointment for New York. You cannot explain some things; you simply let them happen.

I must return to the daily grind, but at least I have something to look forward to. We made an appointment to meet that same week.

From that evening on, we become inseparable. I am living the absolute dream: in love, financially independent, working in an excellent company in the metropolis of the world. What more could I ask for?

Two years later
Return to Athens

After two years of a steady life, we decide to visit Greece with Colette's parents, so that they could meet my parents and siblings.

Beautiful moments! They are all pleased to see us happy. All the signs are there that this relationship will have a happy ending and my parents give us their blessing. They seem happy and proud at my decision.

Inwardly, I want to get married. I have always thought marriage an ideal condition, because this is what I learned from my family and how I imagined it. The thought of giving myself to someone, not for my personal satisfaction but in service to them, is something sacred to me.

We do not spend much time in Greece. Soon we return to America and start making plans for our wedding.

The company president and my future father-in-law calls me to his office and expresses his wish to retire as head of the company and transfer his shares to me, making me his successor.

Material goods were made by people for people, while spiritual goods were made by God for humans.

Normally, I should be ecstatic. Who wouldn't be in my position? Still, something inside me is stuck. Something indefinable stops me from going forward, torments me. For a long time, I am upset, sullen and puzzled.

Friday 12th May, 1989
Manhattan 32nd Street

I am sitting in the small drawing room in my apartment. Opposite me, in the distance, I can see Madison Square Garden. I put on my favorite album, Oxygen by Jean-Michel Jarre, and various thoughts flood my mind. As time passes, I feel my heart aching.

I feel tired and I utter impulsively "Virgin Mary, help me make the right decision."

Human nature is dominated by three tendencies. The first one is the drive for knowledge. This is the foundation of science (good knowledge), the discovery and understanding of the world. The second one is the need for creation. This leads to technology, inventions and innovations of the world. The third one is existential thirst, the quest for a purpose, a destination, and the quest for God. If this third one is only present in an unhealthy manner or not at all, then man becomes arrogant and myopic.

It is evident that I am lacking in the quest for my life's purpose. Also, I feel that I'm living in a time of impressive promises, promises that are filling my soul with intense desires. Disorientation tends to develop as one of the most ruthless powers over us. It has dominated us completely, because it has achieved its main purpose: it has hypnotized our willpower and paralyzed us. We travel in confusion, so certain in uncertainty, so honest in hypocrisy, so real in fantasy… It created human characters without prudence and without clear distinction between easy and difficult, moral and immoral. The ability to distinguish has always been the most demanding human virtue, because it sets the boundaries and saves people and situations, when they stumble.

In this era, the sense of threat, fear, and even panic, starts to take on big dimensions. A wave of unprecedented materialism, hedonism and great vanity is approaching. The world becomes very attractive, but proves tragically isolating. The acquisition of new knowledge is impressive and concepts like logic, agency, the soul, life, and social relationships acquire a new meaning and perspective. The explosion in knowledge and information leads us to the most useful conclusion:

*In the end we are incredibly small,
excessively lonely and hopelessly
instantaneous in cosmic time.*

With all that in my mind, the decision is not late in coming. It is clear, with no room for doubt and vacillations, even though it appears revolutionary and far-fetched.

I decide to return to Greece immediately, the next day even, if possible, to receive the blessing of a spiritual father. This thought came to me like a thunderbolt from a clear sky and struck my heart to make my decision definite.

The biggest battles are fought with the mind, not the body.

I decide to call my brother Spyros in Greece. We are very close; we have both spent quite some time in New York and I believe that he will understand me.

At four in the morning, local Greek time, I inform him that I want to return to our country and want to see a confessor. He is surprised; he doesn't believe me. He tells me that he will call me back at seven in the morning, in order to inform and consult the confessor of my decision.

At five past seven in the morning the phone rings. I am anxiously awaiting my brother's answer.

It was affirmative on the part of the confessor.

I immediately try to arrange the trip through various travel agencies, but it seems in vain, as Easter is approaching and all flights to Greece are fully booked. Later I would find out that that specific day was the Friday of the Akathist Hymn.

After many efforts I manage to find just one seat – in business class – with TWA for next day, a Saturday. I have no other choice. Time is pressing and I ardently wish to return.

I book the ticket and return to Greece. I have told my partner that the trip is due to a very serious family affair and I will be back in a few days. My family is still none the wiser and is not expecting me.

*

"I see a young lady trying to say something. We are listening."

"I have been listening with great interest and, as many of us have faced dilemmas of relevant intensity and cause, we would like to hear your opinion about the struggle between logic and emotion."

"Let us start with the general assumption that inside of us thereexist two fields in simultaneously: the field that calculates and the field that feels. When making a decision both are activated, but simply at different times and usually one is imposed on the other, or at least that is the impression that we get. However, there is no recipe for guaranteed success in making the right decision. Logic and emotion may be considered counterbalancing forces, but they are not. They interact. They complement each other. They co-exist as two variables in the same equation. They seek to solve the same problem.

Emotion usually runs ahead; it shows greater readiness. Perhaps it is more demanding than logic, which functions more analytically, more methodically, more considered. It does not mean, however, that one against the other guarantees greater success in a decision. There are decisions that started at the suggestion of a feeling and, along the way, confirmed to the orders of logic and were deemed successful. Others were finalized in reverse order of influence and also succeeded. Others, however, failed.

In my case, in the case of the biggest decision I've had to make in my life, and which is also the basis for why I am here today, logic tried insistently to impose itself. But my emotions resisted strongly. Personally, I have never ignored the voice of logic. I weighed and evaluated it, but ultimately I took the risk of the heart. Know, however, that the risk is the same, whether our decision is logical or emotional. The doubt about making the right choice will always lurk in the back of your mind. But this is the appeal of risk. The appeal of life. It is just that the better we know ourselves, the better we control the two fields that affect and form our decisions. So, emotion or logic? Or both together? The answer was given ages ago… Know thyself!"

Saturday 13th May, 1989
Athens, Ellinikon Airport

My brother is waiting for me at the airport.

"Welcome! What is the matter with you? Are you upset?"

"Please, let's not stop at home first, but let's go to the confessor directly. I want to consult him about a serious personal matter that has come up."

With the suitcases in hand, we arrive at a small church in the center of Athens. Vasilis told me that there is an old man who reads mass, father Epiphanios, who is also his confessor.

The moment we arrive, Holy Mass is ending. We are led to a small drawing room to have coffee. Most people have gone. Very few remain, only to get his blessing.

The old father appears soon and Spyros immediately introduces me and asks him whether he could see me immediately in private, on my insistence and because of my short stay in Greece.

The father takes me in his fatherly arms and leads me to a small room. I slowly start to reveal what's troubling me, but before I've hardly begun, the old man stops me.

"My son, how long has it been since your last confession?" he asks me.

I am stunned for a short while. "Over ten years, father," I answer. "Since I left Greece, I have not confessed."

"Listen, my son, for God to be able to answer you on the things you asked me about, should you not open your heart to him?"

As he talks to me, his face is shining, his eyes are bright. I feel very relaxed and free in his presence. I don't know exactly how to describe it; it is an unprecedented feeling. My soul is liberated. I am ready to talk and open my heart to him.

I am starting to lay myself bare before him, my experiences and the events that marked my life from childhood up until this time – I don't hold anything back. I do not hide that some things come out with great difficulty. My eyes fill up with tears frequently and I feel that to honestly lay ourselves bare, humiliation is required.

After almost four hours of confession and dialog with the admirable father I embrace him with both arms and tears of joy, like I have never before felt in my life, start flowing unstoppably. I cannot hold them back. My head rests on his chest. My whole being is wondering. *What joy is this? What bliss? Could I be living in a dream?*

He lifts me discreetly. There are tears in his eyes as he beckons me to kneel. His priest's stole covers almost the whole of my body. He puts his right hand on my head and starts to read the prayer of forgiveness. During the prayer, I can feel warmth coming out of his right hand and flood my entire being.

When the prayer ends, I get up and try to utter a few words to express my gratitude, keeping my eyes fixed on the old father's eyes. Before I open my mouth, he speaks first.

"I will tell you something that I've just received as a piece of information. Do not go back to America. Stay at home and give everything you have learned there back to your country, to us who are in need of it. Our country, Greece, needs young men and scientists like you."

For a few seconds I am speechless. My inner being is in turmoil. Two opposing thoughts frantically fight for victory. One is revolting and says: *Are you crazy? Go back immediately to where you have prospects and a guaranteed successful future.* The other, however, is defending itself without compromise, because compromise means retreat, and retreat sooner or later leads to subordination. But ultimately, one must prevail. The father has given me the answer. The decision is mine now.

Obedience bears joy and energy. Obedience because I wish it, not because it is imposed upon me. It is a positive proposition, because you do it willingly. Otherwise, it is not obedience.

"May it be blessed, father" I hear me say impulsively. The joy, enthusiasm and relief I feel are incredible.

"My son, you will find work here immediately, in your country. Indeed, the best kind of work. Do not lose sleep over it."

"Thank you, father, for your love and interest."

An internal earthquake is taking place inside of me and a feeling of freedom inundates me. The others may see nothing, but I see the complete picture. I feel my soul calm down, turn peaceful.

Fear has not prevailed. It was defeated.

Fear is created by the notion of need. People are afraid that they may not fulfill certain needs, both for themselves and for their families. The culture of the society we live in today offers us incredible living conditions for a conventional happiness. It gives us wealth, while simultaneously creating more and more imaginary needs. When people have many imaginary needs, they are also burdened with a constantly growing fear, arising from the incapacity to fulfill all their needs.

A person who is afraid is a person who can be manipulated. Society provides us with technological goods, not as a means of making our life better, but in essence in order to turn us into easily manipulated and easily controlled units. Fear turns to need. Imaginary needs are a continuation of ourselves for the glorification of our ego. The models of our society are formed around material supremacy. Each of us try to define ourselves through the material goods we possess, because unfortunately for our society these have a measurable values. It is through them that we try to distinguish ourselves from the rest. However, imaginary needs do not make us happy. An emotional void covers us which, in reality, does not close with the help of any material conquest. Fear can only be abolished by eliminating imaginary needs. Fewer needs equal fewer fears, and that means greater courage and freedom in our lives.

Can we identify our imaginary needs? If so, then can we reduce them? This is where an all-round knowledge and cultivated intelligence will help to change the direction of our thought. We do not like to sacrifice any part of our welfare. We've turned wholeness into individuality and only care about ourselves, therefore we end up living alone, essentially.

I do not believe that a person alone, without knowledge, without a supportive frame and – above all – without spiritual guidance from above, can succeed in replacing *us* with *me, and* am with *have*.

*

I see a hand insistently raised. So, let's give the floor to our young student. Please!

"I have been listening your speech with interest, but allow me to pause at the concepts of fear and manipulation. We live in an era where both are present in our lives, and in the immediate future our generation will experience them with even greater intensity. Can you please expand upon and delve into these two concepts? Thank you."

"You will allow me to answer with an experiment circulating widely on the internet. It is known as "the experiment with the five monkeys." We put five monkeys in a big cage, feeding them with tasteless meals. After some days, they are fed up with the tasteless food and so we go into the cage, hang a banana from the roof, place a ladder below it, and we leave. There is panic among the monkeys who all scramble to get to the banana, pushing each other out of the way. Finally, after some fights break out, the fastest and strongest monkey manages to climb the ladder and catch the banana. He is holding it in his hand and removing the peel and, just as he is about to have the first bite, we drench him and the other four monkeys who are hungrily looking up at him with ice-cold water. As the monkeys retreat and hide in a corner of the cage, we go in, take away the banana and leave again. The next day, we repeat the same process. Again the fastest and strongest manages to grab the banana, and again we drench him and the others as soon as he is getting ready to eat it. Again the monkeys retreat, and again we take the banana and leave. The same story is repeated for the next two or three days, always with the same ending. Until something changes: as soon as the fastest and strongest monkey dashes towards the banana, the other four grab him and beat him up. So, they avoid getting wet and satisfy their anger at the same time. If another monkey tries to grab the banana, the others' reaction is the same: they beat him up without hesitating. The lesson is now understood: banana equals drenched with cold water. The monkeys no longer touch the banana, because the moment they do so, they will be beaten up by the others.

Days go by and the monkeys make no move for the banana, which we hang up every morning and retrieve untouched every evening. Deep down, they all desire it, but they are aware of the consequences. However, when we replace one of the monkeys in the cage with a new member, as soon as the new monkey sees the banana, he dashes towards the ladder in an attempt to reach the banana, only to be grabbed and taken away by the others. Very soon, after two or three unfortunate attempts and beatings from the four "old monkeys," the new guy learns his lesson: we do not touch the banana.

As soon as the situation is stabilized and peace returns to the cage, we replace one more of the initial monkeys with a new member. The familiar story is repeated, with the new one trying to reach the banana and the others beating him up, including the previous newcomer, as he has now learned that this is the correct response to anybody's attempt to eat the banana. In the same way, gradually, we replace the initial monkeys one by one, until none of those in the first group are left and there are now only monkeys who have never had the experience of being drenched in cold water.

So, what can we conclude from this? We have five monkeys who wish to eat the banana, but don't allow themselves to touch it, or even think about doing so. They don't know why they must not eat it (the threat of being drenched in cold water is no longer present), but they are convinced that it is forbidden. If one attempted it, he would get beaten up by the others, while neither he nor the others would know why. Their collective memory now contains a social rule mandating this specific attitude. For a long time, nobody will dare challenge this law, which determines the protection of the "sacred banana."

I hope that answers your question. I've tried to give you the definitions of fear and manipulation via the results of a proven experiment."

"Thank you, you covered me fully. I hope our generation does not suffer the same fate as the unfortunate monkeys in this experiment."

*

At home, they are all surprised to see me, but still they are happy that, after all these years, we are once again together as a family. I explain the reason for my visit, which will last for only a few days.

I have to be at the office first thing on Monday morning. I have not asked for leave, nor have I mentioned to anyone that I've gone back to Greece. My spiritual father advised me to submit my resignation by phone, referring to serious and sudden personal issues which obliged me to be here. I did so, assuring the company that in a month or so I would return to America to formally submit my resignation and say goodbye to all of them in person.

My family is still ignoring my impending permanent stay in Greece. I am experiencing one of the most difficult periods in my life.

No matter the decision we make, we must stand by it.
consistency in our decisions
shows esteem and respect for ourselves.

Everything happened so fast that I have to provide my family with an explanation. My parents are surprised, but also very happy to have me around for the time being. On the other hand, my siblings are questioning and worried about my decision. They do not agree, especially my sisters. All young people of my age seek a career abroad and suddenly here I am, doing the opposite, leaving everything behind to return to Greece. Very good friends of mine in Greece and elsewhere judge my actions as irresponsible and hasty, devoid of meaning and reason. I am destroying everything in an instant. That's how they see it and they consider me immature.

It is difficult for me to explain what is happening, what exactly led me to this specific decision. I am sure that their approach will be oversimplified and superficial. So, I decide to stay in Greece for some days and organize my next steps.

I start moving. I want to continue my life in Greece. At the intervention of a mutual acquaintance, I am asked to interview for a manager's position at an American technical company with a branch in the Athens Tower on Vasilissis Sophias Avenue. The company takes on many technical projects in Saudi Arabia and the United Arab Emirates.

The father's words are starting to come true. The interview turns to prospects for employment and it has everything I could wish for. I will be paid in American dollars and the salary will be extremely satisfactory and beyond my expectations.

I am called in to sign my employment contract. The employment truly serves to sooth my soul. It makes my self-esteem rise exponentially and simultaneously strengthens my trust in the father's words.

I meet the personnel manager for the formal signatures. As I go out, he tells me: "Do not forget to bring your American passport with you when you return."

I am surprised and say nothing. I have no American passport, just the green card which allows me to be a permanent resident and able to work there lawfully. I have, however, the right to apply for American citizenship thanks to the five years I spent in America as a permanent resident.

I plan to return to America for one month, deal with all formalities, pack my things, submit my written resignation to the company, say goodbye to friends and acquaintances, but – most importantly and most difficult of all – to part from my partner for ever.

Worried and upset, I meet the father once more, who sees right through me.

"My son, what's the matter?"

"Father, I need an American passport for my employment in the new company and I do not have one."

"Don't worry, it will all be ok! Go to America and the Virgin will give it to you."

"It is not that easy. I will have to apply for one at the American State Department, my application has to be approved and, then, I will have to pass an interview and take the oath. The whole process will take at least one to two years."

"Go and you will get the passport."

"These things do not even happen in fairytales, father."

"My son, you do not believe. Go and you will get it."

To be honest, I'm still not convinced.

Wednesday 14th June, 1989
New York

I return to America and my primary concern is to explain my decision to Colette. First, the most difficult things, and then I will deal with my application for American citizenship.

Colette is expecting me at home and starts crying incessantly. I try to calm her down, but in vain.

"Why are you leaving me? I want you to explain. What happened to our plans? What is so insurmountable that we cannot continue our life together, as we had dreamt?"

Words do not come easily. I am mincing my words and am incapable of telling her the real reason. Cowardice, fear… call it what you want. On the one hand, logic dictates that I continue my life in America. But logic is purely a cognitive process with no connection to the heart. Based on logic, it is imperative that I continue my life in America; a totally predictable and secure life.

I consider the unbridled human vanity and addiction to materialism. My upward movement causes passions in me and I need great defenses to resist, which, unfortunately, I do not have.

And where does all this vanity and ascent to the top lead to?

To isolation and greed. On the outside, you may seem happy, but your heart and conscience are the judge. We will always desire something more, and this desire has no end. It is a deadlock and endless. There are, however, no deadlocks if we have guidance, moderation and faith.

On the other hand, mental energy is connected to the heart, to your emotions. We know that to a large extent human decisions give precedence our feelings or are somehow connected to it. My conscience is what tells me to return home. With logic I feel a void, whereas with my conscience I feel complete. One way or another, there is no logic in my decision.

The sadness in Colette's face is a great burden to bear. I wish I could avoid hurting her. Nothing is harder than causing pain where you are normally giving love. My decision does not mean I no longer love or respect her. But it is a decision that, unfortunately, leaves no room for sentiments. It is my responsibility to stick to my decision.

When one loves people, one often has to leave them.

We often have to take our distance from the people we love. Only in this way will we manage to see them more clearly and have a better understanding of their feelings and intentions towards us. Above all, we must not be afraid to lose them or for them to lose us. Risk is a basic condition of freedom.

Emotionally charged, I head straight to the Immigration Office to file my application for citizenship and a passport.

"How long will the whole process take until I am an American citizen?"

"Around two years, sir, from the moment you file the application."

Two days later, Immigration Office

I present the number of my application and plead with them please speed up the process, as I have been employed by an American company in Greece and have to return at the end of the month to start my job. The gentleman serving me, holding my application number in hand, enters a big office with lots of archives in it. He comes out quickly.

"Mr. Ioannidis, unfortunately it is not possible to speed up the process. You will simply have to wait for your turn. I estimate that it will be done around a year and a half from today, at around Christmas next year.

"What? All right, thank you."

I am stunned by the answer. I quickly return to the apartment and immediately call the father to give him the bad news.

"Father, I will have the passport in about a year and a half."

"Be patient, my son, you will get it."

My mind is running non-stop. I am wracking my brain to find a solution and speed up the process.

I obviously lack that most important thing called faith.

I think of asking the owner of a company with which we have an excellent partnership to write a letter for me saying that he's sending me to Greece as his representative, in order to supervise his company's sales in the wider Balkans. "Necessity is the mother of invention," as the saying goes.

With the letter in hand, I once again visit the Immigration Office a few days later, making sure to go to a different member of staff so as not to make a nuisance of myself.

I explain everything to the lady, as I had done the previous time, but this time I present the letter from the company that I will supposedly represent. She disappears for a while into the room with the archives and comes back with a clearly offended look in her face – grumpy, I would say – pointing out that such services are not provided in America without serious cause.

I have lost all hope and am almost on the verge of despair.

Three days before my return to Greece
Company headquarters

The time has come for me to say goodbye to my colleagues and business partners. Their words of love and encouragement are so moving, that they fill me with self-confidence and strength for the rest of my life.

The words that move me the most are those of the company president, who, besides thanking me for my contribution, concludes with the phrase: "If you ever return to America, rest assured that your position will be open for you."

Then, the president personally calls me into his office.

"Colette is very upset by this development. What is so insurmountable that you have to permanently return to Greece? All problems can be overcome. Just solve it and come back. We'll be waiting for you."

I do not give him a clear answer. I am mincing words, again. I'm a coward.

Twice more I attempt the Immigration Bureau with no result. Every day I call the father and inform him about the successive denial of my request. I need to. I feel I am losing my strength, my optimism, but also my faith.

Wednesday 30th May, 1989

Two days before my departure to Greece I get up very early and think I will make one last hopeless attempt at the Immigration Bureau.

Before leaving the apartment, I go to the icon of the Virgin and address her pleadingly.

"My mother had told me that you will give me anything I ask of you, if it is to my benefit. And the father assures me that you will. I am flying to Greece the day after tomorrow."

I start crying. I kiss the icon and, in a last attempt before permanently leaving the States, I head to the public service desk.

It is still early, so the office is not open yet and I am first in line.

The doors open, I enter the big hall and, among the members of staff, I see a new girl. I have never seen her before. Something tells me to approach her.

I explain everything to her, as I did before. I give her my application number and mention that she is my last hope. The girl disappears with my number in hand and, while all the others who served me would come back immediately, taking five minutes at the most, this one takes a long time.

Five minutes go by, then ten, then twenty, and various frightful thoughts cross my mind. But, just as I am beginning to worry, the girl appears with a look of satisfaction on her face, looks me in the my eyes and says:

"This is your lucky day! Today the Deputy Secretary of State is here with us, responsible for cases like yours. I informed him about your case and he wants to meet you personally. Come with me."

A saint is at my side, I think to myself, and I follow her with my head bowed low. She opens a small door on the side and leads me to the deputy minister's office.

It's a huge room, with the American flag on the left and right of the desk and the surrounding walls covered with portraits of almost all American Presidents. As I enter, I notice that the deputy minister stands up and comes towards me, to greet me with a satisfied smile.

*In order to move forward, it is necessary
to have faith in our destination.*

"It is an honor to have people like yourself become American citizens. As I see in your file, you studied in New York and have been working for some years at one of the world's largest multinationals in Eddison, New Jersey. I wish you success in your professional endeavors and that you may continue to work with the diligence that characterizes you for the benefit of our beautiful country. Tomorrow, on Thursday, we are having an oath ceremony and I have registered you as the twenty-first person to take the oath here, in the next room. At the end of the ceremony, all those who have taken the oath will receive a certificate of American citizenship and then you will be able to issue your passport at the end of the hallway."

If someone were to look into my heart at that point, I'm convinced that they would see my gratitude, excitement, and a "God, why do you love me so much, despite my lack of faith?" I want to shout, to cry out with happiness, to take everyone and everything into my arms and kiss them. My joy is indescribable.

I thanked the deputy minister warmly for his interest and understanding for my case, as well as the girl who intervened to bring about this miracle.

Definitive return to Greece

From the airport I go straight to the father.

"Father, I have it! Right here in my hands."

I give him a strong hug. I cannot control my tears, not so much for the miracle, as for this experience that gave me a different view on life that cannot be conveyed.

The start of my permanent settlement in Greece is rather difficult, I must admit. I have to face a change in my way of life, but also the various unyielding temptations and challenges from America which continue to affect me negatively. Our passions follow us wherever we go.

However, deep inside of me, despite all adversities, I feel that I am not alone. Something protects me and gives me the strength, protection and energy to go on. My relationship with my spiritual father, which has became even stronger after my return from America, has played an important and decisive role in my next steps. My life is really changing, and, for one, I am no longer going out until the early hours of the morning as I used to. What I find particularly appealing is the quest for spiritual fathers and having a dialog with them, therefore I use my free time, particularly during weekends, to visit various monasteries in Attica.

Six months later

Coco and her mother unexpectedly travelled to Greece to visit me and persuade me to return. I am taken aback and explain to them that my decision is final. I am not coming back to New York. The situation is difficult and I wish it could've been avoided, but I realize that Colette still has hope that she can persuade me to return. I feel bad for not finding the strength to tell her how things truly are. Perhaps, if I could explain things to her, she would be able to understand and forgive me. I hope time will calm her heart...

My work at the American company in Athens is progressing smoothly. I am coordinating technical projects in the United Arab Emirates. I notice, however, that I'm no longer as excited as I used to be in New York and that my professional expectations have noticeably reduced.

One weekend, the father proposes that I accompany him for a few days to a monastery in the Peloponnese. He hints that I will experience something different there and that the atmosphere will teach me something special.

It is my first four-day long stay at a monastery in Greece after the astonishing experience I had in Athos. The monastery is that of St. John the Baptist in Gortynia. It is built in a cave on a steep rock and looks like an eagle's nest. It is there, in the chapel of St. John, that I first experience a clear calling to the monastic life.

During mass I am sitting in the back, in one of the last pews. There are no other pilgrims in the church, just a few monks on the right and left and two cantors. I remain in my pew, absorbed. The atmosphere has produced an astonishing solemnity and the prayer "Lord Jesus Christ, have mercy on me" comes out of my soul effortlessly, in a somewhat quick rhythm. I feel that someone else is saying the prayer inside of me.

Suddenly, I feel like I have fallen asleep. Strange enough, though, I am fully aware of what is happening and can see and hear everything. At that very moment I hear a voice, very clearly.

"What prevents you from becoming one with that which you admire?"

I jump up, as if I were coming out of the sweet oblivion I had sunk into, and feel an unknown sensation of joy and peace filling me. This is it. My calling to the monastic life at the monastery of St. John the Baptist has been etched very deeply in my soul and is impossible to erase. Nobody can understand me, only my father, who has his own struggles with his illness.

The change in my way of life is becoming obvious, especially to the people who know me well, such as my siblings. I no longer go out in the evenings, but prefer to stay in and read, trying to slowly rid myself of my spiritual crutches.

Above all, I have to deal with the reactions of my brothers, but also friends and acquaintances, who think they are right to question my decision, believing me to be mentally ill and in need of help. This annoys me. I have decided to become a monk, however, deep in my soul, I wonder whether my decision is merely the result of frivolous excitement and will only result in failure and disappointment. It is one thing to play the role of the worldly monk with all worldly comforts, and another one entirely to actually experience it in the monastery, forced to adopt the principles of obedience – for freedom.

Because of his illness, my father is incapable of helping me. So, in order to bolster my decision, I have to find support elsewhere. The situation is not helping me and I am starting to feel mentally exhausted.

In my quest for spiritual support, I ask my sister if father Porfyrios is still alive and whether or not I could visit him. She informs me that, due to his health, he only sees people in exceptional cases. Father Porfyrios loves my sister strongly; he is her spiritual father. I am lucky, because only with her could I see him.

She accompanies me to the same place I had met him the first time, in Oropos, Attica. As soon as we arrive, I realize that the place has nothing to do with what it looked like the first time we visited it. I am looking at a huge monastery with a very big church at its center. The surroundings are well looked after, with trees and many flowers, and there is now a parking area full of cars and pilgrims. I cannot believe my eyes! Exactly what he had mentioned at our first meeting, has now become reality.

The father is very ill and, as the nuns inform us, he cannot see anybody. After many entreaties by my sister, they allow me to only receive his blessing.

I enter his small cell. The father is lying on a narrow wooden bed with his face is turned to the wall, but he is still aware of my presence and behaving as if he had expected me.

"Come, my son, sit down." Without looking at me, he beckons me to sit beside him. "Tell me, what do you want?" He talks with great difficulty and I feel that he is in great pain.

"Father, I do not wish to burden you. I only want to ask you a question. I have decided to become a monk, but inside me I have a fear, a doubt that it might be a simple excitement and that, in the end, I am not up to the demands of monastic life. How shall I overcome the fear that dominates me and does not let me continue?"

He takes my wrist and turns his head. He takes a look at me and I feel it penetrate my whole being; he speaks in a low, trembling voice.

"Not only will you become a monk, but you will also have a long beard. Go now, because I'm in a lot of pain."

When he lies back down, I embrace and kiss him. I leave feeling like the happiest person in the world. Everything has become clear and all of my doubts have vanished. I think that it was the father's look that pressed *delete* and immediately afterwards hit *restart*.

During all this time, excessive love, mainly from my sisters, but, to a large extent, also from my brothers, has served as an obstacle keeping me back from my life's course that my inner voice was dictating to me, producing feelings of guilt, particularly every time they reminded me of our father's state of health.

"If our father had been in good health, he would never approve of such a decision," they kept telling me.

Our father is seriously ill, in hospital, and as the days go by, his health is deteriorating. He is already in aphasia, unable to communicate with those around him and we are informed that his departure from this life is only hours away. The whole family gathers in his hospital room, waiting for our beloved father's death. The emotion of all of us is obvious.

I take the initiative to move next to his pillow, take his right hand in both of mine, as his other hand is full of IVs, and although I know he has no contact with his surroundings, I ask him in front of the entire family: "Father, I have decided to become a monk. Do you give me your blessing so I can leave for the Holy Mount in peace?"

He flutters his eyelids lightly and with an expression of consent he lets two tears flow down his tormented but bright face. That moment marked us all and everybody burst into tears, particularly my sisters, who reacted more strongly to my decision than anyone else.

The departure

I set out on my way to the Holy Mount, without knowing where exactly I will end up and where I will go to retreat. Still, I feel certain that the Virgin will guide me to the place she wants me to go. To be honest, I have taken an internal decision about where I will start.

Every ending is a new beginning. My new beginning would be accompanied by father Ephraim from Katounakia.

As my march on the uphill paths to father Ephraim's kellion[5] in the solitude of the Holy Mount has taken very long and it is getting late, I decide to spend the night in old father Daniel's cell, in the skete of Agia Anna, about an hour's walk from father Ephraim's kellion.

That same evening father Daniel is informed that the monastery abbot will visit him next morning, as he is making a planned visit to the Skete of Agia Anna. Father Daniel proposes to me to wait before leaving for father Ephraim's kellion in order to receive the elder's blessing.

Indeed, the elder arrives next morning, accompanied by two fathers. We meet them at the entrance to the kellion and the elder embraces me warmly. We head into the small reception room of the kellion for the customary treat.

I propose to father Daniel that I prepare the treat and thus leave them alone for a while. I serve coffees, raki, loukoumi and water and, as I am leaving, the elder calls me.

....

[5] A small independent monks' residence

"My son, sit here with us." I sit next to him. "What is the purpose of your visit to the Holy Mount?"

"I have decided to become a monk and it is time for me to find the place."

"Let us talk about your CV for a moment."

Going out, the elder asks one of the fathers accompanying him: "My son, when am I leaving the Holy Mount?"

"In about a week, elder."

He turns towards me. "Well, my son, I will see you before I leave."

I am bewildered. "Yes, elder. I am thinking of passing by the monastery."

My mind is constantly on father Ephraim. It had never crossed my mind to pass by the monastery, let alone to stay there. I do not want to go anywhere else.

Sometimes, the best way to discover who you are is to go to a place where you can't be anything else. Your sacred place. While I know what I am running away from, I don't know what I'm looking for... My spirit is searching, but I know my heart is who will find it.

With this in mind, I depart immediately, taking the path to his kellion in Katounakia. I came to stay in the kellion with father Ephraim. The elder Ephraim and his companions are not unknown to me. I was a guest at his kellion three times before during my almost two-year stay in Greece after my return from America. I am attached to this company – and particularly to the elder, to their way of life, the ascetic mindset and the simplicity that distinguishes them. During my last visit to his kellion, I remember being fascinated by his words.

"It does not matter how long monks fast for," he was saying specifically, "how much they pray or how many hours their mass lasts for. I am interested in something else. Can one of them, even the oldest and in theory wisest one, understand today's troubled people or comfort those in pain? If he can calm down his fellow man and make him feel relief, love life and be grateful to God for it, that is truly a sign of spiritual development."

For this reason, my first choice in my decision to become a monk was to become a member of his company.

After about an hour's walk, I reach his kellion drenched in sweat. I find his small company performing hard labor. I am impressed by the fact that the fathers recognize me as soon as they see me.

"Welcome, engineer from America."

They greet me cordially and offer me the customary treat.

I tell them I wish to stay with them for a few days, if possible, but do not mention the purpose of my visit before I see the elder personally. After all, that is the reason why I asked to see him as soon as possible.

A few hours later the monk with whom I have become friendly tells me that the elder is waiting for me in his cell.

I go to see him and find him half-raised on a narrow wooden bed. His face is shining and his eyes are bright with a clear look. He welcomes me with a thundering voice. I sit down next to him on the side of the bed and tightly take his hand in mine. I feel an unexplained peace inside me and his love penetrating my whole being.

"Elder, I have decided to become a monk and my decision was guided by my first visit to this cell, where we met for the first time some time ago, when I was still contemplating becoming a monk but had not yet made a final decision. I want to stay close to you and to be a part of your company. I cannot think of another place where I can become a monk. You are the first elder I met, loved, and you have been in my heart ever since."

"Stay with us, follow the program of the kellion together with the other monks and I will say a special prayer to find out what our Mother Virgin wants."

A week later

I feel wonderful. I experience the excitement of the monastic life and the monastic community, as the Holy Mount is also called, since I am experiencing something I have never felt before.

The elder calls me to his cell. "My son, you will go to the monastery and live there for the rest of your life. If you do not, I am not responsible for the consequences."

"Father, I know nobody in the monastery. How will I go there?"

He turns and slaps me in the face. I see stars! I feel, however, that it is a slap of love.

"You will do what the Virgin wants, not what you want. First thing in the morning, you will pack your things and leave."

I am sad, but have no choice. As I exit his cell, he tells me in his thundering but now joyful voice: "Listen, I will not leave you alone. I will always be with you."

"Father, will you at least do me the honor of being at my tonsure, if I am ever granted the honor of becoming a monk?"

"Of course. I will give you the tonsure."

The elder's last words bolster my morale. In that moment I believe and feel my initial sadness making way for optimism.

The next day, I take my leave of the brotherhood and slowly get on my way to return to the Skete of Agia Anna, from where I will board the boat to get to the monastery.

Walking down the path leading to the shipyard of the Skete of Agia Anna, I pass in front of father Daniel's kellion, where I spent the night before my departure for elder Ephraim's kellion.

Suddenly, a light goes on in my mind. I remember every detail of what took place in elder Daniel's kellion that morning. His words – "Well, my son, I will see you before I leave" – which had confused me, as I had never thought of becoming a monk or even of visiting a monastery at that moment, are slowly coming true.

We want to be as close as possible to our confessor-instructor. This happens because we feel that he understands us, he aids us, he heals us – as strict as he may be, if he is strict. His charity is freshening, salutary and his strictness charitable.

I arrive at the monastery early at noon. The scenery is incredibly enchanting. In the reception room of the monastery, I am greeted by the monk responsible for hospitality and after the usual treat I ask to see the elder in person. His answer is negative, pointing out that it is difficult to see him personally without an appointment. I mention that father Ephraim from Katounakia is sending me and I absolutely have to see him as per his order.

A little time later, as I have just changed my undershirt and t-shirt which were drenched in sweat from the hike, the hospitality monk returns with a big smile on his face.

"Follow me, please," he tells me. "The elder is waiting to see you."

"But I have not even informed him that I would be coming to the monastery."

"Are you sure? It seemed to me that he knew you were coming!"

We arrive outside the cell. It's a small cell with a tattered mattress rolled up in a corner, a small pillow, a disproportionately large bookcase considering the size of the cell, and a small table with two chairs placed on either side of it. The elder's gaze catches me and I immediately feel something taking place inside of me, a sort of mental transformation. It is something unique, that one can only explain if one experiences it. I feel as if I were going back to a place I already know.

During our first meeting in elder Daniel's cell I was not yet able to understand the meaning of his words, when he told me he would see me before he left.

His loving embrace spoke for itself.

"From today on you are a child of my own and only you will find the way in our brotherhood."

When you discover the Father, your life changes and you can understand it immediately. When you have such a relationship with the Father, he doesn't have to explain much. You will just know it.

This is the Father we all must find. To be able to open ourselves up to him. To have him listening to us, comforting us. To tell him about our problems, our sins, our fears, and to receive from him space in peace. Then we will feel true freedom in our lives.

True love will support us when we slip.

When you have your true Father beside you, the oppression you've felt for so long disappears, because you've discovered who you truly are.

From the very first moment, the monastery offers me this feeling of freedom. The road I've travelled shows me that time, self-discipline, self-surveillance and trial are required for us to be able to adjust to any step we take in our life.

I became part of the brotherhood and truly tasted the greatness of monasticism. I have felt from the beginning that I was an integral part of this family. I was communicating with the fathers and felt them very close to me, like my brothers, as if I had known them for years.

I spend three years as a novice, as the monastery regulation requires. It is difficult for me to describe in words the efforts and the inner struggle I endured during my trial period. In a communal setting, by living together with more than fifty people, each one of whom has his own cross to bear, with all the peculiarities of his characters and his own idiosyncrasies, you are bound to have unfamiliar experiences. But it is mandatory for me to pass through this stage of effort and struggle, this furnace of trial, for me to be able to stand on my own and feel my weakness in all its might.

> *The winner is the one who tames himself,*
> *not the one who defeats others.*
> *The purpose is for you to surpass yourself.*

The elder calls me to his cell. Calm and peaceful as always, but with a relatively serious expression, he tells me:

"My son, during the trial period man is free to choose whether to follow monastic life. The ecclesiastic mystic act of tonsure, my son, will mark the beginning of your new life as a monk and seal the promises you will give for virginity, landlessness and obedience which is a commitment before God and our brotherhood. The assembly of the elders, my son, has now officially decided to accept you as an integral member of our brotherhood, of our family. Two weeks from now your tonsure will take place. We will invite father Ephraim with his company who sent you to our brotherhood, but you, too, my son, can invite whomever you wish to participate in this joyful moment of this unique mystery."

Two weeks later

Holy Mount. Tonsure mystery

Today is a very important day. Perhaps the most important of my life. With feelings of great joy and emotion, my siblings, friends and family members are present for my monastic tonsure, all together. They, in turn, also experience the emotional intensity of this day that is so special to me.

My siblings cannot hold back their tears. From the start to finish, they are all in tears throughout the ritual. They see their brother being reborn, "re-baptized" – and now call me by my monk's name. Friends from America have taken an incredibly long journey to be here today and witness my transformation. Moved, they cannot believe that the direction of my life has changed so much from the course we all followed in Manhattan. My closest friend, George, with whom I am still close, finds it difficult to look me in the eye. He cannot believe it.

My face is lit up by an internal light of emotion and bliss, which strengthens my wish for internal rebirth. Elder Ephraim's presence with his company is a great honor for me as well. It is the fulfillment of a promise he had given me three years earlier, as I was saying goodbye to him in his cell.

Many thoughts wander through my mind. I feel an incredible vindication for the choice I've made.

Whatever one wishes, that is what life will offer him.

What is life? A cloud of steam. You open the lid of the teapot and steam comes out immediately. But as soon as you're looking for the steam, it is gone! That's what life is like, too. It is easily lost. Often, in my free time, I go up from my cell to the forest. There, in the paths of Paradise, I have the chance for a walk, for meditation, for a dialog with God.

Meeting with the "Invisible Recluse"

So, one day, I was walking along the paths of this Paradise, holding in one hand a small stick and in the other a set of prayer beads. It was the time I used to recite the Salutations to our Virgin.

Suddenly, I see an ascetic figure appear from some ruins, a steep precipice, very close to me, at a distance of about twenty meters. It was winter. From what I could see, he was wearing a worn habit, a coat made of hair and a woolen cap on his head. An unprecedented spectacle for me!

As I continued walking along the path, reciting the Salutations, our eyes met. I raised the hand holding the stick and placed the other one on my chest making a little bow. He responded with the same salute.

The precipice he came out from was located on a turn, which means that under normal circumstances he would be ahead of me after our greeting. But he turned before me and I lost him, as on my left there was the precipice and on my right the mountain slope, 3-4 meters high.

I must turn at the corner to get his blessing, I thought. Just a few seconds passed before I had turned, however the elder was nowhere to be found. I started shouting: "Father, where are you?" I took a look in the ravine, but he was nowhere to be seen. On the other hand, even if he had a ladder with him, he would not have been able to climb it.

Suddenly I was overcome by a wave of peace and joy. No fear at all. I thought that maybe God had deigned to give me this blessing, to be able to see at least one of the "Invisible Naked Recluses" in my life. I continued along the path and, after about 20 meters, I abruptly turned round, in case he would allow me to see him again. But, once again, there was nothing. I passed a small bridge reached the other side of the ravine, walking parallel to the path where I had first seen the old recluse. At some point, as I continued reciting the Salutations of our Virgin, I turned my head to the opposite side and I saw the old recluse walking with his head down along the path, a little further from the turn where I had met him. I was moved and my joy was indescribable. I was certain now that the elder was one of the seven "Invisible Naked Recluses."

According to the living and much-proven tradition of the Holy Mount, there are seven "Invisible Naked Recluses" who live on Athos in the most perfect ascetic life and are constantly praying for the world. When one dies, another one takes his place and so their number remains constant. They are called "naked" excessively, as they wear old, torn habits. Additionally, they have the gift of invisibility. This means that whenever they want, they become invisible to humans. Then I realized that their duty was incessant and undistracted prayer to The One they have dedicated their lives to.

> *Only when life has values is it a true life.*
> *Wealth comes through values,*
> *and values come before survival.*

The truth is that I received the message. I tasted the blessing and the memory of the event will remain with me forever. Spiritual life is a spiritual experience that cannot be found in mere words or theories. A personal experience that will follow you to the end of your life and will always give you whatever you lack towards much-desired deification.

The spiritual exhortations of penitence, confession, love, humility, prayer, patience and good thoughts must follow us. It is difficult, but not impossible. It is easy for people to philosophize or theologize about pain. But it is difficult to face pain correctly, when they themselves do not feel a strong pain in their life, when they are not in pain themselves. In this way, we learn to surpass our narrow personal interest.

*

I am surprised to see a member of the Senate raise his hand, probably to ask a question. I was not expecting this. I give him the floor.

"I have been carefully listening to your narration. Your life is a rather controversial one and I must admit that you are beginning to affect my own way of thinking. In the end, what is worth our attention in life? What is truly important? How can we attain personal happiness and balance?"

"Thank you for giving me the opportunity to discuss some crucial concepts. First, I would like to emphasize that life does not provide us with ready-made happiness molds, so long as we do not try to adopt the virtues of kindness, patience, honesty, self-sufficiency, abstinence, and service in our lives.

I asked God to give me strength, and he gave me difficulties to try and face.

I asked for wisdom and he gave me problems to try and solve.

I asked for financial comfort and he gave me intelligence and an ability to work.

I asked for favors and he gave me opportunities to take.

I asked for courage and he gave me dangers to overcome.

I asked for love and he gave me people with difficulties for me to help.

When we offer our help to people with emotional difficulties, not only is the receiver moved, we ourselves cultivate our sympathy too. We take only what we truly need and not that which we desire.

Of what I desired, I received nothing. None of what I wanted. But I've got everything I need. Everything depends on our ability to listen, our consistency of faith and our will to move forward. Happiness and success are two concepts that man invented simply to deceive himself. Absolute happiness and absolute success do not exist. However, in order to experience how each of us interpret happiness or success, we must cultivate the feeling of gratitude. Without gratitude we cannot be blissful, or understand our experiences; this means that we cannot be in the present.

Because in your question you referred to the issue of priorities and balances in our lives, these can certainly not be taught or dictated, but only experienced and re-determined by each of us at different times and with different intensities. So, speaking from personal experience – as that is the only thing I know with absolute accuracy – from an apparently successful life that many would envy, I dared to take a huge step towards my personal happiness. I chose to take that step while disregarding everything else, looking, above all, at my soul and not the vanity of my youth. I wavered frequently, but, finally, I found the purpose we all seek in life and discovered the connection to a higher power.

I often asked myself: "If you do not love what we do, then why did we come to this world? Simply to make a temporary, indifferent passage, leaving nothing behind?" A bold small step may prove to have a huge impact. On the other hand, a step we never took because of cowardice may prove to have disastrous consequences. Let us escape our inner prison and not make the mistake illustrated in the boiled frog syndrome.

The frog, when placed in water that is gradually rising in temperature, will, in response, constantly try to adapt his own temperature to that of the water. If the rate at which the water is heated is 0,02 degrees Celsius per minute, the frog will remain immobile and ultimately die. Any rate higher than that will cause the frog to jump out and escape. When the water is near boiling point, the frog can no longer adapt and tries to get out of the water. This, however, is no longer possible, because he has exhausted all of his energy in adapting to the rising water temperature. What was it that killed the frog? Was it the boiling water or its inability to decide which is the right moment to jump out? What killed the frog in the end was not the boiling water, but his decision to try and adapt his surroundings. In other words, if you would throw the frog directly into the boiling water, he would react by immediately jumping back out again.

The boiled frog syndrome illustrates emotional fatigue, indecisiveness, procrastination and the fear of having to make tough decisions. We therefore must cultivate the virtue of virtues: distinction. The word distinction comes from the verb to distinguish, which means to discern, to see clearly, to decide, or to judge accurately. Distinction is considered a synonym of prudency, wisdom, knowledge, intelligence and discretion. Distinction is what helps us to see that which is correct, to consider what is useful, to avoid extremes and to move in moderation. The absence of distinction in decision-making leads to excess, egoism, fanaticism, criticism, cowardice, and obsession. In order to acquire the gift of distinction, we need effort, discipline, and, most of all, humility. Distinction is the result of maturity and spiritual cultivation. We meet people who fail to achieve their goals and are looking for the reason why. Basically, their failure is focused on a lack of distinction when making suitable decisions and setting priorities.

What has the story of the frog taught us? When a situation in our life is gradually and steadily deteriorating, we often become inert and give up trying to turn the situation around which, unfortunately, causes more discomfort. We refuse to change the conditions around us and, instead, insist on adapting by changing ourselves, exactly like the frog in the boiling water. However, we have to consider which situations are worth adapting to and which aren't. We need distinction, but also audacity in our decisions. In our life we often face dilemmas or are exposed to other people's influences. In both cases the common denominator is bewilderment and internal anxiety. But the ancient Greek philosopher and teacher Aristotle gives us the answer: "Character is the most effective form of influence." If the character is upright and spiritually strong, free from conventional obligations, then it transforms to self-influence and nobody can sway us. Even God allows us free will."

"You will not leave without telling us the reason why you decided to leave Manhattan for the Holy Mount, will you, father? We would all like to hear it."

"As you can see, the answer to such a question cannot be brief. In fact, it would be extremely interesting if each one of us, using what they have learned here today as a listener, answered your question for me. I believe that the different answers would perfectly illustrate the puzzle of my decision, the puzzle of my life. Moreover, each decision we make has its own paper trail, and it cannot normally be one-dimensional. Life is unpredictable. It is not straightforward. We easily fall down, bend, get distracted, excited, succumb. What is important and necessary is that we are capable of getting back up each time we fall. The fall is not the end. It is the trigger of our own resurrection.

In life, the ability of our rectification lurks in every fall.

Life has many downs, but also ups, because people have limits. However, limits are what make our lives interesting and attractive. Imagine if there were no limitations, no reservations, no abstinence… Then all human weaknesses and passions would have free reign to dominate our lives.

I am often asked for my opinion on difficulties and setback and how to manage them. Let us transform difficulty to maturity. The purpose is not to turn difficulty into facility or to neutralize it at once, but to use it to strengthen the person experiencing it. Getting out of a difficulty does not mean that I am forever released of the burdens of life, but that I have become stronger in order to address the subsequent difficulties, which will undoubtedly appear. Difficulty must always be viewed in a positive light. Through difficulties and misfortunes we understand that we are not invincible. Nobody remains untouched by difficulty throughout his life. As humans we are all vulnerable. But this is a blessing. For otherwise evil would only grow stronger in order to prevail over us.

There came a moment, while I was living in Manhattan, when I felt I had everything, and that feeling of absolute self-sufficiency and success made me inwardly tired, it disorganized me. I could not find peace inside. This sense of weakness helps us grow stronger, reconsider, adapt. For our own good, God reminds us of our insignificance in the infinite universe on many occasions. The illusion of invincible strength weakens us, it is a hindrance to our true advancement, in finding our true destination.

So, the answer to your question is the maturity of thought and action. That is what guided me. It helped me to acquire another view of life with my inner eyes, those that are not trapped in other people's lives. Life is an opportunity. With its hardships and setbacks, we discover new skills and capacities with which we gradually develop a different view of our life. Difficulty and hope are interconnected concepts. A critical point for hope is our resistance to difficulty. However, in order to resist, we must be able to change, to adapt. Realizing the need for our own transformation is the beginning of our victory over hardships. We should not forget, however, that the first and greatest difficulties are those we have with ourselves. They are like the hidden scars that we carry on our hearts. It is there that we must focus all of our care.

Regarding hope, let us not hope generally, abstractly, or passively. Between passive and active hope, let us always choose active hope, the one that fuels active endeavor and gives substance to real hope.

To sum it up. In order to move forward, we must have faith in our destination. Without realizing it, our entire life is dedicated to the quest for this destination. Throughout this journey we will often have to face and overcome our limitations. And my personal journey, until I reached my destination, was a continuous confrontation with my limits and weaknesses. A constant conflict, a vibration. However, only on a vibrating rope can one seek and find his balance.

People often ask about our plans for the future. Let us realize that the time we have at our disposal is not infinite. Let us claim new time for our life, then. And because something like that cannot have a quantitative claim, let it have a qualitative one. Man suffers because his internal time is almost exclusively passive, and the result is that he does not feel the need for change. If something activates our internal time and finally changes us, it is the thought and energy we spend to set and achieve that aim. The natural time of a 24-hour day is the same for all of us, but internal time differs depending on the amount of faith and devotion we have for our goals. Isolation helps us to better recognize and utilize our internal time. Only then can we evaluate and balance our internal tensions, resistances and speeds, in order to finally determine our internal dynamism which will help us reach our destination.

I think your questions are making my lecture all the more interesting and I wish we could continue for many more hours. Unfortunately, however, our time here is limited as well, so let us hear one more question before I thank you and say my goodbyes. The last question for today, therefore, but surely not the last resort. Please, I am listening."

"I am very grateful for you to give me the floor and I thank you. We often hear the term "individual responsibility." How easily trodden is this path? And allow me to use the word "path" figuratively, for can I ask... During the first years of your monastic life, did you ever think of turning back on this path?"

Let me start by answering the first part of your question. If the path of responsibility were easy, we would live in an ideal society now, where we would not have to discuss what is self-evident about individual rights, respect and freedom. We would be a balanced society. Individual responsibility is a life attitude, not a coincidental expression. To attain it, all virtues work together subconsciously – consistency, honesty, truthfulness, directness. For the internally responsible person, responsibility does not mean that I take care and prevent, but that I act. Responsibility is an internal process inextricably linked to self-discipline and self-respect. That is why it requires serious and systematic work with ourselves. Consequently, the only entity that can effectively impose it on us is our own conscience. The path of responsibility is demanding and, therefore, difficult.

For me, the path of responsibility showed me my destination and led me to the Holy Mount. Throughout the course of this quest to find myself, my pace may have been quick, sometimes even unstable. I felt, however, that I needed stability. When I finally found it with the help of my spiritual father, I dropped my anchor and my soul became peaceful. That is where I found myself. What had happened earlier in my life was the foundation on which my soul was built. And the foundation, my children, is always deeply rooted in the earth. There is nobody who feels the need to go there and cannot do it...

I am grateful for your attention and time. I hope that you will look up for light and down for humility.

Until next time."

***

Orthodox Logos Publishing

- *De Orthodoxe Kerk: Verleden en heden* – Jean Meyendorff
- *Biecht en communie* – Alexander Schmemann
- *Verliefd Zijn op het Leven* – Samensteller: Maxim Hodak
- *De Orthodoxe Kerk* – Aartspriester Sergei Hackel
- *De mensenrechten in het licht van het Evangelie* – Nicolas Lossky
- *Geboren in Haat Herboren in Liefde* – Klaus Kenneth
- *Hegoumena Thaissia van Leouchino: brieven aan een novice*
- *Het Jezusgebed* – Een monnik van de oosterse kerk
- *Gebedenboek Voor Kinderen: Volgens De Orthodox Christelijke Traditie*
- *Dagboek Van Keizerin Alexandra* – Keizerin Alexandra
- *Mijn ontmoeting met Archimandriet Sophrony* – Aartspriester Silouan Osseel
- *Stap voor stap veranderen* – Vader Meletios Webber
- *De Weg Naar Binnen* – Metropoliet Anthony (Bloom) Van Sourozh
- *Geraakt door God's liefde* – Klooster van de Levenschenkende Bron Chania
- *De Heilige Silouan de Athoniet* – Archimandrite Sophrony
- *The Beatitudes: A Pathway to Theosis* – Christopher J. Mertens
- *De Kracht van de Naam* – Metropoliet Kallistos van Diokleia
- *De Orthodoxe Weg* – Metropoliet Kallistos van Diokleia
- *Serafim van Sarov* – Irina Goraïnoff
- *Feesten van de Orthodoxe Kerk – een Leerzaam Kleurboek*
- *Catechetisch Woord over het Gebed van het Hart* – Aartspreiester Silouan Osseel
- *Naar de Eenheid?* – Leonide Ouspensky
- *Bidden Met Ikonen* – Jim Forest
- *Onze Gedachten Bepalen Ons Leven* – Vader Thaddeus Van Vitovnica

- *Alledaagse Heiligen En Andere Verhalen* – Archimandriet Tichon (Sjevkoenov)
- *Geestelijke Brieven* – Vader Jozef De Hesychast
- *Nihilisme* – Vader Serafim Rose
- *Gods Openbaring Aan Het Menselijk Hart* – Vader Serafim Rose
- *In De Kaukazus* – Monnik Merkurius
- *Terugkeer* – Archimandriet Nektarios Antonopoulos
- *Weest ook gij uitgebreid* – Archimandriet Zacharias (Zacharou)
- *Orthodoxie en de religie van de toekomst* – Vader Serafim Rose
- *Grégoire Krug – Notities van een Ikonenschilder*

- *Our Orthodox Holy Family* – Deacon David Lochbihler, J.D.
- *Prayers to Our Lady East and West* – Deacon David Lochbihler, J.D.
- *The Joy of Orthodoxy* – Deacon David Lochbihler, J.D.
- *The Inner Cohesion between the Bible and the Fathers in Byzantine Tradition* – S.M. Roye
- *St. Germanus of Auxerre* – Howard Huws
- *Elder Anthimos Of Saint Anne's* – Dr. Charalambos M. Bousias
- *Orthodox Preaching as the Oral Icon of Christ* – James Kenneth Hamrick
- *The Final Kingdom* – Pyotr Volkov
- *From Manhattan to the Holy Mountain of Athos* by Thodoris Spiliotis

UITGEVERIJ ORTHODOX LOGOS
www.orthodoxlogos.com

Printed in the USA
CPSIA information can be obtained
at www.ICGtesting.com
LVHW091314101124
796163LV00005B/352